Recollections

of a

Young Desert Rat:

Impressions of
Nevada and Death Valley

By Daniel Cronkhite

Published by
THE SAGEBRUSH PRESS
P.O. Box 337
Verdi, Nevada 89439
June, 1972

This book is dedicated to
HER
wherever she may be

Acknowledgments

●

As *Recollections of a Young Desert Rat* began to take form, i.e., the transformation from mental notes to words on paper, the author realized the project would be greatly improved were help obtained from someone in the literary world. He then turned for assistance to E. I. Edwards, renowned desert bibliographer, a gentleman he holds in the highest esteem. Mr. Edwards, author of such works as *The Enduring Desert* and *The Valley Whose Name Is Death,* patiently edited the manuscript and offered constructive criticism. There are however, several passages in the text which may very well raise the eye brows of those in the upper echelon of literature, but these irregularities may be attributed solely to the radical independence of the author.

Foreword

●

While visiting a huge second-hand book store in the San Francisco area a few years ago, I was impressed with the sight of more than half a million volumes stored and stacked about on the many shelves. Standing alone in the middle of one room which housed writings of Western Americana, I imagined the many authors suddenly taking voice and clamoring to speak — voices of history unleashed from the barrier of time for a fleeting moment, only to clash in a din of confusion. But no, the room was indeed quiet — the books stood in silence, void of life, the hushed atmosphere broken only by my muffled footsteps on the thick carpet. As I browsed and thumbed through the various titles, I felt as though the room possessed a holy air, for the writings were serious expressions of people who are a part of our Western heritage.

It was this book store visit that rekindled my long standing dream of writing a personal and autobiographical work, and something deep within urged that I do so before too many more years slipped by.

A short time later I began work on *Recollections,* grabbing a scratch pad and jotting down notes at random, or turning the light on in the early morning hours to catch a thought before it raced away. And so, for several years now, notes have been accumulating at an alarming rate until recently the project nearly got out of hand. Only by resisting my lethargic nature and pounding the typewriter late into the night has the effort reached this stage.

You will find the following pages to contain episodes written in a variety of moods. They reflect what I have felt and seen. That you will enjoy *Recollections of a Young Desert Rat* is my sincere wish.

> — The Author,
> Somewhere in the Desert.

CHAPTER ONE

●

The Making of a Desert Rat

Born and raised on a two-acre "farm" in the San Fernando Valley of California, I grew up in an atmosphere of limited ranching as we raised chickens, geese, pigs, rabbits and a number of garden crops. Our home in the north central portion of the Valley harbored a definite flavor of country life, for during my childhood our property was surrounded by a dairy, large fields of agricultural products, groves of walnut trees, and a paradise of dense growth and sand known as the Pacoima Wash, a virtual haven for adventurous kids and wandering hobos. But the press of a growing Los Angeles steadily advanced our way until one day the dairy was ploughed under and replaced with a housing development, the agricultural center transformed into Panorama City, the walnut trees felled by hungry chain saws, and the Wash stripped of its vegetation and molded into a naked gully of asphalt, concrete and chain-link fencing. And with the changes came the laws which accompany progress; and soon our humble operation was declared out of line with the manufactured world about us, until our parcel of land now stands nearly void of all traces of yesterday.

The seemingly endless years in grammar and junior high school are not ones I can recall with fond memories, for they were marred with countless battles and teen-age warfare with cliques of tough kids who delighted in administering bloody noses and blackened eyes. Instead of wearing my collar turned up and tinkering with hot cars, I labored about our acreage, delivered newspapers for four years, and established the ground work for a home print shop — a dream which formed at the age of 13. Then, somewhere along about 1956, my family took a short vacation to Death Valley and there, in all that vast beauty and peaceful silence, I discovered the wonders of the desert. An unexplainable enchantment possessed me and from that day on I have found the desert to be a huge classroom, a region of penetrating solitude and rich history.

Having taken a sip of desert wine, I found the crush of city and suburban living most unpleasant and I set about preparing for the day when I could make my home in the country of sagebrush and sand. At 16 years of age I acquired my first printing press, an ancient Chandler & Price platen of 1899 vintage, and began publishing small booklets concerning my new-found love. High school was a vast improvement over the earlier days of schooling, for in the hallowed halls of Van Nuys High I found countless hours of enjoyment in the old but delightful print shop. Those days were good, for despite the usual rigors and set-backs prevalent in a student body of several thousand teenagers, I found a purpose in life, a goal that pointed to the publishing of historical material. Two great instructors, Arthur Sparks and the late William Chambers gave much encouragement.

Social contacts were kept at a minimum in my high school years, unwittingly now that I think of it, for my thoughts were on a different plane and I found no interest in climbing the ladder of social prominence. Every opportunity found either my Dad or a friend and I traveling into the desert in search of the secrets which linger there. Upon graduation in 1961 I seized the offering of a job on a weekly newspaper in Tonopah, Nevada, and there spent several months learning the trade, climbing sun-drenched hills, exploring rickety old mine shafts, and listening to the music of old timers telling tales of yesterday. Experiences gleaned during my stay there were many, some of which are discussed in the pages of this book; but with the sweet words of a girl back home filtering my way via the mail, and the desire to acquire necessary equipment to operate my own print shop, I left the desert with firm resolve that one day I would return.

When I came back to the San Fernando Valley, the land of my birth (it did seem like a different country), I found not the ideals of my plans, but rather a bottomless pit of looking for a job while floundering about on the tide of urban blight. The girl I returned to see also had a goal, one a bit different than mine, her definition of paradise being marriage. She spoke often of "us" and her desire for a cozy home in one of those cliff dwellings people call apartment houses. "But what about the desert?" I wailed. "I must live either in the desert or in a mountain community — a place free of the rat race." "But Danny," she cooed in a seductive voice, "We can always *visit* the country on a week-end, or *sometime*." But the thought processes knew well that if I ever yielded to this urging I would be reeled into the mesh of the "system" and consumed like so much fuel in the furnace of industry. I pictured myself caged within the limits of an apartment house, skidding off the walls and witnessing my wife wearying of my anguish. So I refused the brightly painted package of a city marriage and watched the girl, with sadness, exit my life.

The entire period of my 19th through 22nd years of life, spent in Southern California, was gripped with a gnawing desire to amass the proper funds to effect a speedy departure; but always there was something to prevent my move: a need to purchase an item that required extensive time payments (printing presses, etc.), friends to whom one becomes attached, and a number of other diversions. My brother meanwhile found the city to his liking and pursued a career in the professional field, rising rapidly in the ranks of his choosing. But as for me, I felt impelled to leave the city to those who liked it.

So for some four and a half years I stood before a machine flipping buttons and switches and making adjustments, deep within the gray walls of a huge aircraft plant. I watched employees of many years moving about like automatons in a vast characterless system, their personalities and thoughts placated by seven cents an hour raises and fringe benefits. The daily grind and the monotonous plodding soon became unbearable. The words of Longfellow lingered in my mind: "Our hearts like muffled drums beating a funeral march to the grave." One day I suddenly leaped to my feet and screamed "Enough!" The time for the move had come. "It's now or never," the inner voice said.

And so, without the grubstake I had intended to create, I readied for my return to the land of far horizons. I remember well the words of my father as he spoke of the security in the good job I was forsaking and his vain attempt at having me postpone my departure. "At least stay until you acquire a five-year pin" he pleaded. "Five-year pin! What on earth is a five-year pin good for?" I queried. He overrode my question with the proud statement that he had three pins commemorating his five, ten and twenty-five years of service and that I too should earn at least one. I then asked, "Where are your pins now, Dad?" Hesitantly he replied, "They're somewhere in my dresser drawer." For me the sealing wax had been applied. My decision to move was final.

With that I succumbed to the beckonings of my conscience. The choice has since proved both painful and rewarding; although the experience and knowledge obtained these past few years has been invaluable. No formal system of education could have ever offered the wisdom that has been thrust upon me during my tenure in the school of hard knocks.

I am reminded of the process employed in the hardening of steel, for the procedure entails the execution of two extremes — incredible heat and cold. In the commercial production of such metal, ingots of steel are subjected to temperatures in excess of 2,000 degrees, then dropped into vats of water or sub-zero refrigeration systems; in blacksmithing, matter is extracted from the glowing coals of a forge, ruthlessly hammered and twisted into shape, then plunged into water. These methods produce either a strong, useful product or a useless hunk of fractured metal. Thus it has been said that for the character of the human being to be strengthened, an individual must be able to face and endure a number of trials and tribulations, else he may become an object of indifference caring only to satisfy his sensual desires. I felt the strong possibility that the apathy so prevalent in our society today could easily overcome me were I to remain a resident of the sprawling Los Angeles Basin.

So breaking away from the world of jammed freeways, blaring televisions, high-rise buildings of glass and steel, and the endless sea of the faceless crowd, I embarked upon another way of life.

I fled to that bleak hill-top mining town of Tonopah, Nevada, the spot where I labored five years earlier, and — as before — I went to work at the local newspaper. I had plans for making the job a permanent one and calling Tonopah my home, but the situation in the dank quarters of the composing room soon became strained as the conditions were anything but good. My work included the making-up, printing, and tearing-down of four weekly newspapers, type setting, floor sweeping, and a multitude of other assorted duties, all time-consuming and menial. One segment of the job required the melting of lead, pouring of ingots and casting of stereotype mats in a room which measured approximately four by ten feet. Here in what was unbelieveablly cramped space, I manned two melting pots and a lead-cutting saw. As the loads of Linotype slugs and old castings softened, liquified, perked and broiled, the temperature in the small room soared in excess of 140 degrees (I checked) and the air became stifling as the small exhaust fan whirled away in vain. Drenched with sweat and riddled with splinters of flying lead fragments from the saw, my lungs gulped mouthfuls of gaseous fumes. Peering through the window of the door into the rest of the shop I wondered if I were a mad scientist obsessed with cauldrons of stewing poison or a victim in a gas chamber. My hours were long, often 60 and 70 hours a week — but with only 40 hours pay, and many evenings were spent alone in the musty 50-year-old shop racing to beat the ever-present deadlines. Printing has long been a "professional love" with me, but the spirit longed for an opportunity to express itself with work of a creative nature, not the repetitious drudgery of newspaper printing.

During this period my long standing interest in Nevada history intensified, and whenever finances permitted I added choice out-of-print books to my growing collection. Spare time found me engrossed in research, and when the winds of winter began to howl I spent considerable time hunched over a typewriter and surrounded by volumes of outstanding reading material. It was an enjoyable pastime, one which seemed to harmonize with the historically rich country in which I lived.

Somewhere along the line I grew a beard, with no real purpose in mind other than to satisfy curiosity. I was aware that men not so long ago (of both humble and important status) often supported healthy crops of whiskers and were respected in allowing nature to have its way. A beard, somewhat of a natural phenomenom if one thinks about it, is not an item of fashion obtainable at the local haberdashery, but rather is a gift from the Creator. I have always believed if care is exercised in sporting a "hirsute appendage" a certain masculine pride can be derived. However, as my own endeavor began to develop I became aware of a word which was new to the English language, that being "hippie." Considerable harassment and crude remarks soon filtered my way and became rather frequent from certain members of society, but in time my beard became a part of me and I was not conscious of any "oddment."

While my beard growing was purely for personal reasons and void of any political nuances, I soon realized the American public was being subjected to huge doses of propaganda and seathed with prejudical opinion. Beliefs are many and varied in these vexing times, with a great deal of pseudo-religious and political theories overlapping one another, until now it is nearly impossible to say just what is right and what is wrong. Perhaps this is one method employed by "them" (whoever they are) to bring about the downfall of our country, for surely "organized confusion" and the destruction of respect for our neighbor (and ourselves) will certainly further national chaos. It seems apparent only a renewed faith in God can save this great land, but then again many Americans don't even believe in the Almighty, so obsessed with knowledge without wisdom are they. Ours is a complex age, one where evil all too often is permitted the ascendancy and the innocent and ignorant are cruelly punished.

January of 1967 started off on the wrong foot when some midnight merchant helped himself to two brand new tires and wheels from the bed of my pick-up truck. This unfortunate event occurred on New Year's night; it blew any optimism I might have had for a better new year. A few days later the newspaper job completely soured and the spirit of wanderlust cried for new adventure, so I accepted a job of swamping and truck driving in the "outback" of Nevada. The government was engaged in the sinking of a series of test holes so that Uncle Sam could fracture some more atoms, and the firm for which I worked supplied the drilling companies with loads of chemicals and supplies. A whole new world unfolded before me as a co-worker and I bounced along in a 10-wheel "Cornbinder" (ask any truck driver what a Cornbinder is) across wide lonely valleys to little camps isolated in remote corners of the wilderness. We worked hard as we wrestled with hundred pound sacks of strange chemicals which encrusted and ate at our skin; but even with the dust that lined our throats like chalk and with straight shifts of 36 and 48 hours we felt good. Tired and exhausted, but somehow triumphant. Roads were carved out of virgin terrain by bulldozers, and strips of cloth tied to bushes and stakes driven in the ground guided us to new drilling sites. Even the carcass of some range animal served as road information, for when being directed to a new operation we were instructed to turn left at the dead cow.

And then in all its squalor of heavy rainfall, snow, sleet and axle-deep mud came winter. Often we knifed our way through pea-soup thick fog and groped to the dim lights of a drill rig, the tower reaching a hundred feet into the sky like a beacon, and looking for all the world like a polar cap weather station. It was a rugged and wild existence, but one rich with satisfaction.

One star-twinkling night, when the temperature was considerably below zero, my companion and I found ourselves returning from a delivery in Monitor Valley, a huge expanse of emptiness north of Belmont, the old Nye County seat. With our rig now void of a load and the drive wheels without the necessary weight, we struggled for hours in the frigid night air trying to get up an ice-slickened dirt and gravel grade. Shoveling frozen muck, securing brush for traction beneath the huge wheels, and toiling with massive tire chains, our sweat-soaked clothes froze and stiffened, and my beard (a wonderful insulation piece) was caked hard and adorned with several inch-long salty icicles. Exhausted and with blood-shot eyes, we finally reached the summit about midnight and descended into the ghost town of Belmont. Its collection of old snow-covered buildings, huddled in eerie silence beneath a full moon, leered at us like mystics of another age.

But as the job became an enjoyable one of lusty adventure, someone in an office somewhere erased what was to have been a two-year contract after only a few months, and I was suddenly unemployed. It was about this time that I heard of an opportunity to establish a print shop in Arizona with a man who operated a weekly newspaper; so, in due course, I made my way south to investigate.

The persistent urge to operate my own shop had been simmering for a number of years so, when I heard that the "chance of a life-time" for such an operation was available, I became eager to look into it. Subsequent reconnaissance showed that the Arizona town in question was a growing vacation and resort area, and a visit with the proprietor of the weekly newspaper netted a volley of enticing stories which promised a most lucrative business. Always being of a trusting nature I agreed to a partnership without the signing of any legal papers, and proceeded to move the machinery I had accumulated while living in Southern California from the home of my parents to the Arizona desert. With the last few dollars I possessed I hauled my shop, piece by piece, across several hundred miles of barren land; but because the weight of the presses and accompanying supplies was too great a load, the truck's transmission soon ground into a mass of broken gears and had to be replaced. Eventually I established my shop in the building of the small town newspaper publisher and awaited the mountain of job printing my associate said was available. The onslaught never came. It in fact never existed, except in the mind of the promiser. All too soon it became apparent the move had been one of folly and the sweet dreams of success had taken wings and fluttered into the sunset. The situation was bleak for I was caught in the strangling grip of poverty, only to have that surpassed by my associate's inaugurating a series of clever maneuvers in an attempt to take possession of my equipment. Work was scarce in all that blinding heat; but just when it looked as if all was lost I secured a ditch-digging job that enabled me to collect enough money to pick up my shop and run — no easy task.

Not wishing to return the machinery to Southern California I looked far and wide for some ideal country community to relocate. In the northwest portion of Nevada I found the pleasant hamlet of Verdi and began the process of moving there. The distance between the heat-plagued spot in Arizona and the little town at the base of the Sierra Nevadas was nearly 600 miles, and for two weeks I motored back and forth hauling and dragging various items of graphic arts machinery. With little capital and no help in moving I tired of the long hours and back-breaking task but, hoping the future to be better, I plodded on. On one haul a 3,000 pound press shifted and created many miles of apprehensive driving, but stopping on the edge of Tonopah, the wonderful Dominic Lambertucci (spoken of later in this book) fired up his huge caterpillar tractor and with a cable pulled the load back to proper position.

The last object to be moved was my house trailer,

a heavy well-built structure some 42 feet in length and approximately ten years old. It had been moved to Arizona from Tonopah with the aid of Tom Morse, a truly great individual who expended much time and energy in my behalf, but I could not bring myself to impose upon him again for he was a very busy family man laden with enough personal problems. So, renting a vehicle of a "beefy" nature, I started the process of moving my home by myself. A few miles down the road I was struck with the realization that the truck was inadequate for the load. Traveling by night to avoid excessive traffic, I piloted the straining truck with its cargo up steep grades in first gear and rolled along the flat lands at incredible speeds up to 25 miles per hour. With the anxiety brought on by the deeds of the questionable businessman, and the nerve-wracking ordeal of transporting the heavy machinery over so many miles, I bordered on the edge of physical exhaustion. North of Las Vegas I pulled into a roadside rest, inspected the massive load, then slept for an hour.

Feeling better after my brief slumber, I again started up U. S. Highway 95, rolling along slowly but surely. But hiding in the shadows was a demon of grief preparing to deliver a devastating blow for, unknown to me, tragedy lurked like a bandit in my course ahead. Some seven miles into Nye County, near the turnoff to Mercury (the AEC Test Range) the road narrows from a divided highway to an older two-lane affair and descends in a long gradual slope. Down this grade my truck-trailer rolled gathering momentum far faster than I was aware of. The sinking sensation of moving too fast seized me, and I gently applied the brakes; but as if the Devil himself was in charge a freak wind suddenly swept across the highway and the cargo behind the truck began to whiplash, mildly at first but uncontrollably within seconds. I thank God for having the road clear of oncoming traffic, for the truck and trailer careened wildly down the two-laned asphalt road as I grappled in vain with the unmanageable steering wheel. Then the split second of eternity flashed before me and my mind was jammed with a thousand unanswered questions. I was yanked violently back into reality when the nauseating roar of the trailer flipping onto its side penetrated my senses. Helplessly I rode the stricken rig as it skidded along in a shower of sparks and flying gravel, coming to a jack-knifed halt with the truck resting on the right front wheel, the trailer tongue and hitch twisted like salt water taffy.

Scrambling from beneath the mountain of clothing and boxes which had been on the seat beside me, I pushed open the truck's door and dropped some four feet to the ground. There before me was a most horrible sight. On its side and with the tandem wheels still spinning amidst a swirling cloud of dust, the trailer lay like a huge animal gasping its last breath. Grief swept over me and my very soul screamed for relief as I beseeched the heavens for an answer. The tears could not be held back for, to me, all was lost — but suddenly a vivid picture flashed before me — that of a soldier dodging machine gun fire in a Vietnam rice paddy, and I could almost hear the unidentified infantryman offering to trade places with me. It was another lesson, a test to determine my ability to accept hardship and trial. But the pain and utter hopelessness was still there, and in a dazed condition I stumbled about viewing the stricken craft.

Heavily I eased my weary body to the sloping ground of a roadside culvert and waited for the approach of some form of life. Ten minutes of silence passed before a lone automobile on the highway came into view, slowed and stopped. A few minutes later a number of vehicles had arrived and many people were on the scene peering at the strange spectacle. Eventually a highway patrolman arrived and went about the routine of obtaining accident data, asking questions in a voice which signified he had seen it all time and again. The carnage had completely blocked the highway, which necessitated the detouring of traffic through the roadside brush and sand. A tow truck was summoned to upright the trailer, for despite the smashed front end, broken windows and shattered interior, a good repair job could have made the mobile home liveable again. But grief had not finished its work with me. When the tow truck's cable was attached to the framework of the trailer and the slack taken up I witnessed in horror the ultimate destruction as the frame separated from the body and the entire contents spewed onto the ground. It was like viewing the execution of a friend. I could hardly believe my eyes nor my sense of hearing when I heard the towing agent declare nonchalantly, "This sort of thing happens every time. Har har!"

When the patrolman at the scene decided not to write me a citation for obstructing a public thoroughfare, a glimmer of thankfulness sparked somewhere in the depths of my wearied chest. There was also one passer-by who distinguished himself from the small number who paused and gawked at the wreckage — a gentleman from Colorado City, Texas. His name was Travis Turner, and I shall never forget that man. He sensed my plight, spoke a few reassuring words, and handed me a $20 bill. The money was badly needed, but it was the man's actions and the kindness that were as an unguent to my tortured soul. But a hidden ace of spades was dealt by the tow truck owner when he unceremoniously presented me with a bill of $150 for "services rendered." I stammered a broken reply that I couldn't possibly pay such a sum, for my entire cash resources, including the Texan's stipend, totaled approximately $30. (He made no reference to the damaged vehicle that had been completely ruined.) My debt was settled when the trailer base and tandem wheels, laden with the refrigerator, stove and water heater were carted off to the agent's place of business.

In a state of shock I secured a broom from the wreckage and swept the highway clear of broken glass. Later, when everyone had left the site and I remained alone, I milled aimlessly about the underbrush picking up scattered personal effects — and in the process obtained another profound experience. Stuck in a bush, its pages fluttering in the breeze, was a copy of James R. Moffat's *Memoirs of an Old-Timer,* a booklet I had printed for a resident of the ghost town of Rhyolite,

Nevada. In retrospect I thumbed through the pages, thinking of Moffat, the two editions of the book that had been printed, and of the many graphic art projects I hoped to produce. Shortly thereafter I learned Mr. Moffat had passed away a few days earlier and his funeral was held in the old cemetery near Rhyolite at the precise time of my crash. An awesome coincidence to be sure. I wonder if Moffat's spirit, freed of the bondage of this physical life, witnessed my nightmare.

The badly bent right-front wheel on the truck was eventually replaced and I piled what salvagable goods remained into the bed of the vehicle and tied down the load. Leaving the bones of my home to bleach in the desert sun, I started off toward Verdi, determined future events would be a triffle better. As I drove north, a lone coyote loped across the highway before me, and halted a short distance from the road and looked my way. He was a pitiful sight, gaunt, with hair all matted, obviously the victim of dire circumstances — and I found myself saying aloud, "It's pretty rough, ain't it pal?"

Some years before I had met and maintained regular correspondence with a college youth who had an interest in Nevada history. When it became apparent I needed a location for my shop, the two of us agreed to a limited partnership, took steps at establishing a small book selling and printing business, and moved my equipment into an old building in Verdi. The structure which housed our struggling enterprise was an old one, but solid in construction and capable of serving the immediate needs. It did however, lack such luxuries as electricity and heating. These maladies proved to be a serious stumbling block, for requests to the landlord (a prominent Reno businessman) to have these services made available were futile. His secretary handed us the stock answer that he "was not available."

The young man who entered the business venture with me lived in palatial splendor in one of the better housing developments in Reno, having the bulk of his bills taken care of by a handy source "back home." My situation, since the loss of the trailer, was of a different note, for I carved an existence out of the dark and cold confines in the rear of the shop building. Fresh off the Arizona desert, my blood was still thin as ten weight motor oil. Before I had time to recondition my system, winter made its initial appearance in the form of a nasty cold wave which sent temperatures to the zero-and-five-degree mark. How well I remember the nights I had my bed covered with every available scrap of clothing and still tossed and turned in miserable slumber. Such an experience, while uncomfortable, turned my thinking to the pioneers of the West, for they often faced situations of discomfort far more severe than any of my misfortunes. As electricity was not yet available, I was not only unable to operate my shop, but even reading and writing became a task, for a candle was all I had. We have all used candles at one time or another, but prolonged use of them as an only source of light etched a deep message on the slate of my being, for I found the light would flicker and border on extinction if a page of a newspaper was rustled or a deep sigh emitted.

When it became obvious the landlord was not going to remedy the sorry condition of the building, I took steps toward having electricity and propane piped in. After several weeks of exhausting and seemingly endless effort, we were rewarded with the musical sound of an operating press. Immediately a few small printing jobs were contracted so that the bills could be paid and some food stockpiled. Then I began work on a personal endeavor entitled *Death Valley's Victims*, a book composed of hand-set type. However, I had hardly started when another dark cloud passed over. An inspector of the county arrived one day, gave the building the once over, and piously announced in the tone of a warden pronouncing the death sentence, that the building failed to meet the county's thousand and one codes and rulings, and promptly issued a decree which halted all operations. I made another attempt to contact the landlord, and was successful in reaching him by phone; but the outcome was vastly unsatisfactory for, when I told him of the problem at hand, he muttered something about my going to the place of eternal damnation and slammed down the receiver.

With all channels of income cut off, I went to work for a newspaper in Reno and earned enough to sustain a living. While newspaper work usually commands good wages, the hiring executive of this organization chose to ignore all my printing experience because it was of an individual nature and not union sanctioned, hence my wage was one-third of scale. Within a few months time however, I realized my independent spirit did not mesh with the crass world of men engaged in the deadly game of politics, as were those about me, so I continued to scan the horizon for that golden opportunity I was sure to find one day.

Awaiting some constructive action by the landlord, I continued to live in the shop building in Verdi, and while conditions were touch and go, I met some truly wonderful people. I can speak of postmistress Maxine Anderson, artist Zona Clark Walker, and real estate agent Florence Marsh Martin with the highest praise, for these fine people provided a friendship so desperately needed during a period of raw and trying times. When one receives the clenched fist of fate pounded into his face repeatedly, bitterness can easily set in, but the kind actions of a few can soothe even the greatest of injuries.

My partner meanwhile tired of the delays and setbacks created by the landlord's duplicity and suggested we hold back rent payments until the owner took steps to bring the building up to the county's specification. Mr. Landlord, upon renting us the building, had assured us the structure met all official regulations and was ideal for starting a small business such as ours. The withholding of rent funds brought action in the form of a nasty letter from the Reno businessman, threatening us with a number of dire consequences. My partner, who earlier indicated he might drop his interest in our project, agreed with a friendly handshake to "stick it out" so that we might fight the problem together; but I returned one night from my newspaper job to discover he had cleaned-out the stock of books we had placed on sale, and hot-footed it to points elsewhere. A few days later the portly land-lord (the very figure political cartoonists use to illus-trate selfish men) obtained a court order seizing the entire contents of the shop building, including my equipment, library, personal belongings, and even a motorcycle. The shop was padlocked and I was turned loose to wander the streets.

The picture was again bleak, as it had been before; but this time my nervous system was feeling the pres-sure of so much unfavorable luck I wondered if I would become the fractured piece of steel spoken of earlier in this treatise. A friend provided a place for me to sleep on the floor of his cramped house trailer, and within a couple of weeks I was able to locate a small house on the edge of Reno. At this same time, some 500 miles away, my tireless gray-haired mother, who has worked hard her entire life, struggled and scraped together enough funds to loan me so I could post a bond and have my property released from the clutches of the very greedy and unscrupulous landlord. A long legal battle ensued and a date in civil court was scheduled; but on the eve of the hearing Mr. Landlord developed cold feet and dropped his black bag of charges. I then underwent, once again, the fatiguing process of moving my shop from Verdi into Reno. Once settled I continued work on my Death Valley publication. In time it was released in a limited edi-tion, received good reviews by authors of Western Americana, and soon was out of print.

The publishing of *Death Valley's Victims* was an inspiring effort for the results were quite encouraging.

I have plans of producing other works of a desert nature, not based on a lust for quick wealth but as an artistic expression (true graphic arts is indeed an *art*) and in the hopes someone finds enjoyment and information in them. We all are the recipients of disappointing set-backs at one time or another, and this scribe has received his just share, hence my publishing efforts of late have been curtailed. But with the help of the great and powerful Creator I will recover the fumble and strive for another first down and an eventual touchdown.

My observations and wandering these past few years have been an era in my life. I've felt, seen and witnessed much. Many times I've sauntered through the peaceful streets of comfortable country villages and lounged in the shade of a desert oasis. I've also spent hours gazing at the ducks and gulls floating about on the waters of the Truckee River, and in speechless wonderment viewed colorful sunrises and settings in Death Valley and the Nevada desert. And with misgivings and deep thought I have watched homeless men on skid row wander about aimlessly in the fog of their misery. There is no one all encompassing answer to these various aspects of life, but rather it is a giant stage where we are permitted to prance about and perform our tricks for a while. It is a serious and sombre talent show, with the Great Judge viewing it all. This is how I see it — just one more voice and opinion in a roaring sea of countless individuals.

CHAPTER TWO

•

A Winter Night on the Desert

The unexplainable enchantment which encompasses the desert country of California and Nevada has long been an intriguing lure to me, one which has drawn me into its vastness time and again. While living in Southern California I often found the press of city life intensifying and would then look to the desert for a change. Times such as these found me throwing some provisions in the back seat of my nifty 1948 Chevy, shaking the clammy hand of the city from my shoulder, and fleeing into the desert for a season of rest, introspection and writing.

Often these journeys led me to the crumbling ruins of Rhyolite, Nevada, a ghost town not far from Death Valley. My friends Mr. and Mrs. Herschel Heisler (the former is now deceased) consented to my lodging in the old caboose near their train depot/home in the abandoned mining camp, and I would spend several days there. The ancient rail piece, a relic of one of the defunct lines which once served Rhyolite, has long been a favorite with me, and I have slept there on many occasions. The interior of the wooden coach possesses a musty odor which serves as a mild intoxicant to history buffs like myself, and the old stove with the pipe running the length of the living area produces a rare warmth, especially when the icy winds howl outside.

Here in the late hours of the night I would read and write by the light of a lantern and lose myself in much the same manner a Tibetan Monk might. It was a blissful interlude in the life of a struggling scribe, but it did have its moments of trial too; one in particular which still burns in my mind was a Christmas Eve. Separated from family and friends by choice, the thought processes milled relentlessly of "that girl back home" and of happy families enjoying Christmas Eve together in their cozy homes. My fabricated world of solitude was shaken.

As the hour neared two in the morning, I fed the stove some more fuel, extinguished the lantern's flickering flame, and crawled into the warmth of my blankets. Lying in the darkness I mentally rearranged sections of a story I had labored over, then permitted the mind gradually to saunter into the fields of leisure and memorable events of times past. It was at this moment that I reached out of the bed and groped for a battery-operated short wave radio I had brought along. The only link with the rest of the world, I gave the on-off switch a turn and the transistorized device immediately produced a collection of warbling sounds. The frigid atmosphere of that winter night jammed the air waves with a thousand voices and sounds; but, as I tampered with the selector dial the undulating sounds, first far off and fading, came in sharp and clear. How I can still remember, nay, still hear, the sound of "Little Drummer Boy" and the glorious music of Christmas.

It was a strange Christmas Eve; a lonely one, to be sure, but a rewarding experience quite unmeasurable. Slumber rapidly approached and I turned off the sounds of the outside world and dug a bit deeper into the blankets, for it was bitterly cold, and the efforts of the old stove were soon erased by the night air. Pure golden silence surrounded me, with only the deep sighing of the night-time wind making a sound.

Times such as these are priceless; they are part of my *Recollections.*

CHAPTER THREE

•

The Desert — A Summertime Inferno

It was on a steep hillside between the Keane Wonder Mill and Mine that I found a peaceful afternoon of pure lethargy, one I still remember with clarity. Attracted to this quiet spot of sun-baked rocks and bare land, I sat soaking up the rays of a warm but comfortable September sun. I came alone to the huge theatre named Death Valley, and on a stage some 130 miles long I viewed the beauties of nature at work.

Lulled into a pleasant slumber by the warmth, I drifted between sleep and consciousness and watched the shimmering heat waves dancing far below me. The Valley lay broiling in the sun, and it was so utterly quiet that a high pitched sound could be heard — the sound of silence. But lo — the stillness was abruptly shattered by a resounding noise of metal clanging against metal, the report filtering down from high up in the canyon. Three times the spine-tingling noise sounded with several sets of echos following, completely baffling my senses. Then again, silence. I sat upright in wonderment, beseeching the vast canyon walls to explain the strange and weird report. As if in answer, a lone raven soared mystically overhead, the only other living creature I saw that day, save a few lazy lizards. The shining black feathers of Mr. Raven glistened in the sun as he floated on an air current. Then, swooping near me, he emitted a series of rusty squawks as if in protest to my invasion of his domain, and then he glided down-canyon and out of view. Not another sound other than my own movements was heard that day. It was as though my feathered visitor had created the alarming racket by knocking loose some rocks which crashed onto some of the old mining equipment scattered about.

I continued my motionless vigil on the barren hillside and watched the sun steadily move across the sky and eventually dip behind the towering Panamint Range. The salt flats and alkali deposits on the Valley's floor, and the grotesque mountains and canyons all developed first a copper hue and then a deep purple advancing into twilight. The glistening cornice atop the Panamints glowed with magnificient zeal, and the closing day produced numerous panoramic displays. Finally the sun's rays became less and less effective and the great Valley of Death dissappeared into a veil of blackness. Still I sat at my vantage point until the first stars of the night made their appearance in the heavens and the lights of distant Furnace Creek and Stovepipe Wells glimmered and danced in the ever moving atmosphere.

Here in an area which once was engulfed in the noisy process of men blasting and drilling into the rocky hills for rich ore, I found absolute serenity and quietude. And here I remained for several days viewing and experiencing the desert.

The Keane Wonder mining district is located in the Funeral Range on the eastern side of Death Valley. A huge mill and tram-way terminus stands at the base of the mountains on the edge of the Valley proper while the main mine and smaller workings are located high up in the hills some 3,000 feet higher in elevation. Massive tram stations built of huge timbers dot the hillside from the mill to the mine, standing muted and eerie as if frozen in time, their cables still stretching over the 300 foot deep canyons and gorges. A foot path winds and weaves up to the mine, but few people who attempt the trek complete the long journey up the steep grade. I gazed at the rusted ore buckets hanging from the cables, wondering at the events which one day brought a grinding halt to the clattering works. Notorious for the bewildering heat, the workings are said to have been a place a man could always find a job. Caves and prospect tunnels still harbor signs that men lived in their shadows in an effort to escape the awful heat.

But now the area was void of human activity and I beheld an aura of timelessness. I felt a strange force which seemed to transfix me into a suspension of reality, I almost forgot that another world of freeways, glass and steel lay on the other side of the surrounding mountains. Then, from far below in the darkness, I saw in the sky above the tell-tale vapor trail of a jet plane caught in the sunlight. I suddenly remembered the age in which I lived — not the days of twenty-mule teams and buckboards, but the age of jets and computers and credit cards and universal problems.

* * *

July of 1964 found us in Death Valley. It was hot, very hot — and exceedingly dry. My friend Gary and I had come to learn of the heat; and, from the great but stern instructor called Nature, we learned plenty. And of this heat I feel compelled to write.

We had chosen the Chloride Cliff area as our classroom, and enroute we stopped at Stovepipe Wells. We found the place deserted like an abandoned movie set, and I marveled at the complete lack of human life as compared to a November rally of the Death Valley 49ers' Organization. A fierce wind, mindful of the breath of hell, raked the landscape and raced across the porch of the general store. The thermometer in the shade registered a cheerful 119 degrees despite the fact that the hour neared six in the evening. A dry wit inside the establishment greeted us with some such encouraging remark as his dreading the warm season, due to *start* a few weeks hence.

Proceeding on we traversed Daylight Pass, turned off the highway onto one of those dandy back-country dirt roads, and motored to the ruins of Chloride City, not encountering another individual in the entire journey of several miles. We found a spot protected from the ever-recurring wind, unloaded the pick-up, and established a camp of sorts. As twilight approached, great clouds of bats emerged from old mine tunnels and caves and filled the sky in search of food; the warm evening air produced a host of animals and insect life as they began their nocturnal wanderings.

Now bachelors are not usually noted for their culinary skills, and over an open fire what knowledge they do possess often goes up in smoke. But the two of us managed to manufacture an edible substance which sustained life somewhat, whereafter we retired to our respective bedrolls and laid atop them in the pleasant evening air, witnessing the indescribable beauty of the heavens in its overwhelming array of stars. A number of shooting stars highlighted the night but sleep finally drew the show to a close.

Firmly secured in the arms of slumber we blissfully snored into the early hours of the morning when, about 2 a.m., a freak thunderstorm happened along and deposited its entire stock of moisture on us within a period of three minutes. The ground fairly steamed from the unexpected rainfall as the clouds proudly marched on into the night, and once again the brilliant stars returned in all their radiant glory.

Sunrise occurred in clear warm skies. The rocky landscape and its sparce vegetation stood in muted silence, as if in anticipation of phenomenal happenings. Some four-legged "critter" had visited our camp during the night and cleaned up all the food scraps we left lying out for just such hungry creatures. We filled our canteens, slipped into loose-fitting long-sleeve shirts, donned our hats, and started off into the vastness of the Funeral Mountains in search of old mines and isolated workings in an effort to see firsthand what a summer sun was like.

We soon found out.

The country was rough and rocky, but the ground upon which we walked was aged mica which fractured and broke beneath our weight. Descending a steep mountain slope we jogged, plunged and slid into the ever increasing heat, the latter becoming greater with the decreasing altitude. All along our route were signs that men had toiled in the district not so long ago, all in that endless search for wealth. The dust rose to the sky and the loose rock rolled and slid downhill with us as we plowed into the heat.

Approximately two hours lapsed when we came onto a small and complete mine and mill site that had not felt the violent impact of marauding adventure-seekers bent on destroying all they encounter. The little camp possessed a well-built ball mill, a chemist's laboratory complete with bottles of chemicals, a small tramway, rock cabins and one very healthy chuckwalla lizard who permitted us to snap one photograph before darting off into the rocks. We poked about the ruins like a couple of schoolkids, but were careful to leave things pretty much the way they were. The two of us never cared for wanton destruction.

Dated material lying about indicated the operations stopped with the advent of World War II, and in an oversized mine tunnel we found a couple of old bunk beds and a stack of late 1930 magazines. The sun had reached the mid-way point in its journey across the sky and the heat blanketed the canyon with stiffling intensity; so, in the tunnel we sought refuge. The tunnel was cool and relaxing, and lying sprawled about on the bunks we feasted on a make-shift lunch and browsed through vintage literature reading of Hupmobiles and prohibition. Sort of a bunker it was, away off in the desert, miles from the demanding forces of society.

The hour soon reached mid-afternoon and the two of us concluded it was time for the main lesson in this school bordering on the inferno. Like two boys knowing punishment awaited us, we ventured forth from the sanctuary of the tunnel into a Death Valley summer and immediately felt the sledge-hammer blast of the cruel heat. Without exaggeration I can truthfully say I believe the temperature that day was above the 130 degree mark for the air which we breathed was remarkably like that of a sauna bath. The lungs labored and gasped for fresh air and after we had been exposed to the full wrath of the sun for a time the jagged peaks around us became blurry in the shimmering waves. Each armed with a walking stick, we moved onward and upward. The massive hill which we joyfully skied down upon that morning now loomed before us like a Mount Everest void of snow. We plodded up the steep incline, slipped in the shale, blithered delirious thoughts of pretty girls frolicking around a tree-shaded swimming pool, wondered of man's fiendish lust for gold, and of our foolish determination in seeking adventure. The swirling dust enveloped our bodies and formed rivulets of mud in our sweat, with the oven-dry atmosphere extracting what moisture the dust did not claim.

Progress was exceedingly slow, and at one point Gary became sick to his stomach and a muscle-gripping cramp seized the thigh of my right leg. We stopped to rest, not sitting down for fear we wouldn't rise again, it was unbearably hot. A thousand feet beneath us lay the dormant ruins of the mine we had visited, and as our labored breathing subsided, not a sound was to be heard. With fixed gazes staring blankly at the haze-shrouded Valley before us, a gentle breeze — as if from Heaven — awakened us from our state of stupor. Feeling somewhat better we turned and clambered up the hill. Farther up the steep face we stopped again, this time for a sip of water from our canteens, but were disappointed to discover the expectant cool liquid to be nauseatingly warm. The sun glared off the glittering mica and our eyes narrowed to mere squints. We "spat cotton" and ran our sleeves across our brows, then stumbled on toward our camp.

It was late afternoon when we reached our little camp, bone-weary and exhausted. Sagging like a deflated punching bag in the shade of our truck, I thought of the many unfortunate victims who had became trapped or lost in the confines of this place with no hope of reaching "camp" — but wanting only to find some shade and water. Our trek was uncomfortable to be sure, but nothing like the pain and suffering of those who had fallen victims in days gone by.

* * *

And then there was Bullhead City, Arizona.

A mere 30 years ago, before my time, this area of northwestern Arizona was a piece of very harsh roadless desert, but now Davis Dam stands proudly in the middle of the Colorado River, beckoning thousands annually to the man-made mecca of a fishing and boating paradise. Vast villages of mobile homes and other housing projects have been developed along with a number of businesses, until now the once bleak spot of desert offers a wide variety of recreational diversions. Retirees and investment seekers have found the locale to their liking and the population has been steadily growing for several years.

However I was lured there on what was promised a solid business venture, a situation which soured and resulted in a mountain of personal hardship. In the ensuing process of struggling back onto my feet, I experienced raw desert living which etched some very deep scars on my soul. It is a great place for those wishing to frolic in the sun and motor about on the river and lake, but to attempt the task of eking out an existence without a sizeable grubstake can prove to be a painful ordeal. Dragging my trusty trailer down from the frigid northland of central Nevada (the generous efforts of Tom Morse of Tonopah helping immeasurably) I established house keeping just as summer began its seasonal bombardment, and immediately felt the stark difference in the sub-freezing weather of Tonopah as compared to Bullhead City's broiling temperatures. Parked in the sweltering sun, the old trailer accumulated such terrific heat that canned goods spoiled, the refrigerator's motor ran continuously, and the interior of the shelter became practically uninhabitable. One evening proved particularly hard to sleep, and checking the thermometer I was chagrined to observe a reading of 106 degrees at midnight.

Due to the proximity of the Colorado River, the air for miles on both sides of the major waterway was thick with humidity which mixed with the fantastic temperatures for an end result of intolerable discomfort. Those persons blessed with sufficient capital installed refrigeration coolers in their homes without delay, but many endured the scorching elements sans any mechanical aids. The less expensive swamp coolers used in dry climated areas proved grossly inadequate as such systems merely added more moisture to the already humid surroundings.

Spare time found a good number of people floating about in the cool waters of the Colorado with only their nostrils and top-most part of the head protruding — much like a rhinoceros. Even saw one youngster beat the heat by completely submerging himself and breathing through a hollow reed.

Thunderstorms of terrific magnitude rocked the area intermittently, deluging the country in heavy rainfall and bombarding the sound waves with the loudest thunder I have ever heard. These summer storms made a point of visiting the community in the middle of the night, arriving with little or no advance notice. The flashes of lightning were exceptionally brilliant as the storm broke directly overhead, the cannonading thunder resembling jet aircraft breaking the sound barrier. One such storm ignited the thirsty creosote and mesquite growth on the Nevada side of the river which resulted in a raging fire that burned out of control for days.

One wickedly hot day I observed an interesting spectacle in the form of a band of Indian youths nonchalantly raking a field clear of rocks. I found them armed with ponderous steel rakes, toiling in the midday heat amidst a cloud of swirling dust. Muttering among themselves, they were seemingly unaware of the ungodly heat that had forced most everyone else off the streets. I later learned they were engaged in a government sponsored *self-improvement* program.

When it became apparent the business venture I had engaged in was not going to materialize, I began to look about for some form of employment so that I could amass enough coin to effect a speedy departure. Jobs are not usually plentiful in the desert and because it was the month of July I found the situation even more unfavorable. Repeated efforts to locate work were futile and the financial picture worsened with the passing of each day. I eventually hit rock-bottom on the monetary scale and crawled in the trench of poverty for a time, when finally the enchanting words that laborers were needed at a construction site filtered my way. I was immediately on the scene ready to go to work.

The job was a dandy. A small crew of men, of which I was a member, was detailed the chore of clearing a sun-baked field of defiant brush, rolls of rusted barbed wire, and firmly planted fence posts.

Also, we had to level an old shack and dig trenches. In an effort to beat the torrid heat we were instructed to begin work at dawn; but even at that hour we found the job site engulfed in a pall of clammy and sticky heat. At the beginning of the job we normally halted work around noon and continued in the late afternoon and evening, but as a deadline had been established we were soon forced to stay with it the entire day.

The weather had been expectantly hot all summer long, but one period was particularly bad when the evening temperatures did not dip below the 100 degree mark for more than seven days. With the heat came an unusual onslaught of humidity, and I can remember all too well the day the official report logged a reading of 127 degrees with 75% humidity. That day like all the others was one of work, and like members of some chain gang we were in the field laboriously assaulting a line of stubborn fence posts with demonic vigor. The atmosphere was chokingly thick and oppressive, and breathing was painful and sporadic. Knowing that to drink cool water would be comparable to pouring water on a hot stove, we selected hot coffee and tea, but it provided little comfort to our crazed minds and throats.

It was about one p. m. on this sweltering day when the invisible hand of nature reached down and belted a number of us peons in the face. Shoveling stifling dirt and debris from a ditch, I looked up to see the pale-white face of a co-worker staring blankly at me. A moment later he collapsed in his tracks. He was hauled like a sack of meal to the meager shade of a cat-claw bush where he remained several hours doubled up in pain. Not long after, a series of cold chills and goosebumps raced up and down the back of my arms and neck, and I too developed the ghost-like pallor that gripped my fellow worker. The boss of the crew, making the rounds of his subjects, stopped when he came to me, lifted my hat, made a fast observation and ordered me to the shade for a few minutes rest. I staggered from the ditch like a drunkard and flopped on the lee side of an old shack and remained motionless for over two hours. The rest of the men deserted the project for the day, and the field lay shimmering and empty like ground zero of an atomic bomb site.

The job was finally completed and I made good my escape to another point on the map of the Southwest. Enroute I tripped over another painful situation — as told in depth earlier. Just one more perplexing lesson in the School of Hard Knocks.

* * *

Death Valley's mysticism has lured men into her hot embrace for over 100 years, with the hope of locating some lucrative mineral usually being the reason for venturing there. It was for years a massive uncharted region of barren sun-baked mountains, salt and borax deposits, and a place which mysteriously consumed the lives of foolhardy adventurers and prospectors.

The sun-baked mountains and the ooze on the Valley's floor are still there, but today's modern traveler with his smooth riding air-conditioned automobile and insulated dwellings has found the below sea-level pit to be another Palm Springs for several months of the year. Indeed, the fall, winter and spring months offer ideal weather for the recreation minded man, and oft times the facilities at Furnace Creek and Stovepipe Wells are hard pressed by huge crowds of urban dwellers in pursuit of relaxation. Ah, but the infamous months of May through September have always been and still are a season of unbelieveable heat — especially for the unfortunate soul who finds himself traversing the region on foot. Tomesha, the Indian word for Death Valley seems apropos, for it means literally "ground afire."

Despite all the warnings and advice of "summertime dangers," man has repeatedly entered this "cauldron of death" on foot in the midst of scorching heat to prove himself capable of overcoming the impossible. These little-publicized endeavors were of no import until the nation's news media focused our attention on one such adventurer in 1966 — a Frenchman who had set out to conquer 102 miles of cross country terrain during the month of July. Sponsored by a soft drink firm, Jean Pierre Marquant of Nice, France, toiled for some eight and one-half days scaling Telescope Peak, slipping and sliding downhill to Badwater, over the salt pinnacles of the Devil's Golf Course and across the sand dunes to Stovepipe Wells. His was an amazing feat, for the temperature during the hours of his walk never dropped below 110 degrees. Marquant said he undertook the trek to prove to Frenchmen and other Europeans that "there is still adventure in America. Europeans, especially those from my country, have some strange ideas about the United States," he said. "Many go to New York. It's strange. They hate New York so they hate America. They never really get to know the people or the many wonders of this country." The then 28-year old Frenchman's efforts were well covered by the writings of an elite corp of newsmen and photographers who, waiting at appointed rendevous', gathered the latest comments of the hiker as he stopped for rest. Michel Aubert and Miss Colette Reumont, two compatriots, served as a support party for Marquant by establishing "stations" and dispensing refreshments and changes of clothing. It has been estimated a hiker would consume some 21 pounds of water a day under such conditions, making the attempt by a lone individual nearly impossible without assistance.

I was drifting around the Valley during this time and found Marquant on the day he completed his trek. Snapping a few photographs I sensed the man's eager desire to flee the area — which he did one hour after the completion of the hike. He returned to Los Angeles and related some of his experiences at a press conference.

Marquant's marathon created wide-spread interest among other such persons lusting for public acclaim, for a rash of hikers and joggers descended into the Valley during the summers of 1967, '68 and '69 performing all sorts of Herculean feats. Several of these heat-defying aspirants were successful in their quest while others felt the doubled fist of the Valley's punishing effects and were forced to give up the cause. For the most part these post-Marquant enthusiasts received some mention from the wire services, but none came close to gaining notoriety as did the clever Frenchman.

There was, however, one individual who completely missed the spotlight in a vain attempt to establish himself a hero, and in his lack of knowledge was bitterly disappointed. For a time immediately following the days of Marquant, the Death Valley-Nevada area was graced with the presence of a vagabond who addressed himself as Wheelbarrow Tex, so named because of his habit of carting his entire worldly possessions around in a dilapidated one-wheeled contrivance. Tex had heard the furor created by the hikers, and had even observed some of the cars of the press chasing after news-making individuals. With all this slowly soaking in, Tex finally succumbed to the irresistable urge to join the crowd and share in the tasting of glory.

Finally plotting a course of action, Tex crammed his goods onto his unusual mode of transportation, tied down all the gear and departed the sleepy ghost town of Rhyolite one hot summer day. Lacking the finesse of professional adventurers such as Marquant, and not schooled in the proper manner of relating his experiences, Tex used file-like adjectives in describing his ordeal, and mumbled that the "damned journey was hotter than the blankety-blank gates of hell." For over a week Tex trudged along, first pushing the load up steep Daylight Pass then holding back the vessel on the long descent into the Valley proper. Plodding along he envisioned throngs of newsmen waiting at his finish line of Stovepipe Wells, but stumbled into that settlement on an unbelievably scorching day only to find the site void of any humanity, save a few die hards inside the local store firmly entrenched in front of a swamp cooler.

Tex, sadly disappointed, vainly attempted to impress the local citizenry with his accomplishment* and beseeched them to summon the news services. He witnessed first hand, not glory and fame, but the power of the press and managed news — or rather, the lack of such.

---

* Accomplishment indeed! Tex's arduous journey was made without any of the aids available to Marquant. Tex carried all his own water, ate what non-perishable food he had with him, slept on the ground, and suffered the elements as did those in the early days of Death Valley.

CHAPTER FOUR

●

Those Cold Icy Fingers of Winter

While working on the local newspaper in Tonopah during 1961-62, my place of lodging was a room at the rear of the home of an elderly lady who had lived in the same location since 1913. The old but well-built house was on the eastern end of town where a magnificent view of the mining camp was afforded. In the days before I acquired my dandy '48 Chevy, I walked the approximate mile to and from work, and experienced classic examples of thunderstorms, blazing heat, rampant wind, a few utterly delightful days, and *last but not least, winter.*

I vividly recall some of those crisp evenings in December and January—the ground was frozen hard, and the sound of my feet crunching the snow still rings in my ears. Those memorable times were invigorating to be sure, but some of the less fortunate creatures of the area suffered greatly during these cold snaps. One particular period which hosted below zero temperature readings for a week, found some of the dogs—which were compelled to spend the night outside—yipping and howling the entire night, so great was their discomfort. My heart pained for those poor animals when

I heard their cries of anguish, but I was powerless to act. I vowed never to treat an animal in such a fashion should I ever own one.

It was one of these evenings that I found myself tromping home through knee-deep drifts of snow, wondering if my lungs might seize-up like a set of motorcycle pistons. My exhaled breath seemed to hang in the air, as if frozen; I wondered if this was Tonopah, Nevada, or the Yukon Territory of Canada.

My room was separated from the main part of the house by a screened-in service porch. For want of a better place to keep the key to my room, the landlady, then near 80 years of age but spry and vigorous, deemed the vegetable bin of the refrigerator (which was on the porch) as an ideal location. She wanted it at hand as she often busied herself by tidying up my room.

Nevertheless, this particular evening found me bounding onto the porch after my hike up the hill from town. Kicking the snow from my boots, I peered at the thermometer by the door, and I believed my hair stood on end when I saw it registered at 22 degrees below zero. "Outtasight!" I mumbled to myself, or words to that effect, as I made my way to the refrigerator for the key. Opening the door, I was greeted by a blast of refreshing warm air, and before the storage box I stood a good ten or fifteen seconds soaking up the warmth. I was indeed chagrined when my numb senses finally realized I was obtaining heat from an ice box. Thawing out somewhat, I then figured the atmosphere around me was considerably below zero, as attested by the thermometer, and that the refrigerator manufactured a temperature of approximately 40 degrees above zero. With a difference of some 60 degrees, I found it rather comfortable.

* * *

The beautiful little community of Verdi, Nevada, some ten miles west of Reno on the California state line, was my home in late 1967 and 1968. However, I found myself eking out an existence in a building which lacked heat and electricity. The result of a crafty land-lord, that winter was indeed one of endurance and chattering teeth.

One miserable night found me covered with every blanket I owned, plus a jacket and numerous articles of clothing, and a few sheets of newspapering. I awoke in the early morning hours while it was still dark, to find myself thirsty, so reached for a canteen of water I kept by my bed. Winter displayed itself in grandeur when I found the water frozen solid.

* * *

Death Valley is noted for an abundance of unusual oddities, and one winter evening in the late 1950's na-ture shared one of these mysteries with me.

The weather had been unusually cold for the Valley, and the higher elevated country to the north, west and east was mantled in snow. Enjoying an evening of in-tense clarity and sharpness near Stovepipe Wells, I was startled to see a profusion of color — what appeared to be huge searchlights, moving about over the Funeral Range and Grapevine Mountains. At first I believed it to be the work of the Atomic Energy Commission over in Nevada, but then realized the moving rays of *red* light, somewhat like huge piano keys, extended across the entire range of mountains, and that no man-made object could do so. Joy swept over me, when my thinking apparatus suddenly proclaimed, "That's the Aurora Borealis!" Some may doubt that the Northern Lights can extend so far southward, but I know what ever it was, man did not create it.

The heavenly network of unmeasurable entertainment broadcasted its dazzling array for some ten minutes, then gradually diminished. It was late in the evening, near eleven o'clock, and as the red "keyboard" vanished, the vivid stars resumed their usual but no less spectacular nightly exhibit.

It was a rare treat for a desert lover — one I'll always treasure.

CHAPTER FIVE

•

Ambassador of a Mining Town

Recently a married couple I know was in Las Vegas to view the glittering lights of the "Strip" and make an attempt at getting rich overnight, the latter endeavor not being very successful. Making their way from casino to casino, they noted with interest a rather large gathering of people in the lobby of one of the newer and more elaborate establishments. Their curiosity was aroused, for the gambling areas lacked the usual crush of patrons — the bulk of the crowd had filtered to the lobby. Elbowing their way through the throng, my friends were pleasantly surprised to find the center of attraction to be an old miner complete with flowing white beard, back-country clothing, and time worn boots. This couple, as did the many others, found this figure of days gone by a refreshing change from the constant hubbub of crap shooters and obsessed slot machine addicts. The colorful prospector was delighting those within earshot by tales of his encounters and experiences during Nevada's early days.

When this incident was related to me I immediately thought of another such old-timer, a fantastic character who resides in Tonopah. I refer to one Andy

Anderson or, as he is widely known, Mizpah Andy. Now Andy did not unearth a bonanza, nor did he set the world on fire with his own exploits, his claim to fame lies in his representative spirit. Possessing a fine white beard, and dressed in the garb of the typical desert rat prospector, Andy tells of the desert and of the days of yesteryear. For those who are interested and will take the time to tarry, true desert entertainment is theirs for the asking, for Andy produces a line of desert chatter the likes of which is a rare treat. Mizpah Andy is an ambassador of this great region.

Andy's early days were spent in a diverse manner. Born in 1888 he dabbled in real estate, was a bank teller, and saw World War I as a sailor in Uncle Sam's Navy. His native state is California, and it was there he spent the majority of his time. While yet a single man he went to work for an investment firm which had poured huge sums of capital into mining properties in Goldfield, Nevada. He was sent by the firm to investigate their holdings and to report their potential. Surprised was he, and the company, when it was discovered the investments were all on paper. The details have long since scattered to the wind, but the swindling loss his company suffered no doubt was the work of George Graham Rice, a clever manipulator of money who spread his cunning operations to all points of the globe.

By no means was Andy's activities restricted to a clerical nature, for he undertook prospecting in Mexico, Arizona, California, Oregon and Nevada. He also toiled in an asphalt plant for a while and, after his marriage in 1933, he spent some time on private ventures in Goldfield. World War II sent men to the industrial centers of America, and Andy joined in the aid of his country by laboring in some of the major ship yards on the coast.

The year 1954 marked his arrival in Tonopah, where he sought retirement. Rapidly becoming a part of the community, and feeling the spirit of the mining camp atmosphere, Andy soon became the legend he is today.

To supplement his income, Andy became a "general representative" of the town and the Mizpah Hotel. This establishment, which operated continuously since 1901, kept its doors open for some 64 continuous years, but a change of ownership in 1965 saw some questionable operations by Eastern investors, and bankruptcy soon followed.

With the entire matter shrouded in a veil of mystery, the "Easterners" fled in a cloud of dust to their part of the world, and the former owners, after overcoming considerable red-tape, regained the landmark and opened the doors once again in 1966 — whereupon Andy's former position of "ambassador and general welcomer" was reactivated.

While in the employ of the Mizpah Hotel, Andy greeted travelers and tourists on the sidewalks of Main Street, briefing his new friends on Tonopah's rich history and passing out souvenirs, compliments of the Hotel. It has been a familiar sight for years to find Andy on Main Street discussing some topic with a passer-by, tamping tobacco in his pipe, while a contingent of elite canines — all members of Andy's welcoming committee — lay sprawled about at his feet.

Although he has slowed down a bit now, the late 1950's and early 60's found him in Death Valley engaged in the annual Flapjack Burro Race, attending historical celebrations in various desert communities, and in the thick of Tonopah's parades and shindigs. Sharing the limelight for many years was his Mexican burro, Tequila, the two of them adding much color to many desert hoe-downs.

However, few people know the *true* Andy, the man who enjoys good books and can converse on many profound subjects. Those who have paused long enough really to visit this most interesting individual have discovered a brilliant and knowledgeable gentleman of the highest calibre.

Invited to drop by his home one day, I accepted Andy's invitation and stopped off at his place on the eastern side of the Tonopah township. From the front his abode looks much the same as those around it — a wooden structure boasting a picket fence, and shaded by a couple of fine trees. But the day of my visit was in the dead of summer so, upon greeting me at the gate, Andy escorted me to the backyard where an entirely different world confronted me. Here I found a profusion of various botanical rarities, unusual specimens for the United States, and particularly the Nevada desert. As if touring the lush gardens of the green northland, Andy pointed out his prize agricultural gems. Would you believe a New Zealand tomato *tree*? Or how about a cherry *bush*? Hard to fathom perhaps, but these plants and an array of others thrived as though Tonopah was the horticultural paradise of the world. A giant sunflower prospered nicely as did some 30 or 40 rose bushes. The yard supported a number of healthy elm trees too, which provided welcome shade from the desert sun. Andy's wife appeared and the three of us found some chairs and enjoyed home made ice cream. One could easily imagine Andy's yard being an oasis for the weary traveler — a place welcomed by any man coming off the hot desert.

Our conversation touched on many subjects: the desert, our fellow man, religion, animals, and poetry — the latter catching me by complete surprise. Andy is an accomplished poet, a desert poet that is, and — with a little prodding — can rattle off example after example. True desert literature too, untarnished by the editors of a staid New York publishing house. Without showing any signs of forgetfulness Andy, with a twinkle in his eye and a hearty laugh, rolled off several verses when asked to do so. A couple I enjoyed were:

> Spring house cleaning time is here again,
> For the shack ain't been cleaned since God knows when.
> New curtains are hung by the window side,
> For the better the uncleaned portions to hide.
> Floors are swept clean — but not under the bed,
> 'Cause you can't see there 'less you stand on your head.

Another ditty he served up was entitled *Passport to Heaven,* and goes like this:

> I dreamed I went to heaven.
> I heard Saint Peter say:
> Tell me of some kindly act
> That you performed this day.

Well, I fed some homeless doggies, and
Patted each dear shaggy head.
That's good enough for me boy,
Come in, Saint Peter said.

The above poem portrays Andy's love for animals,
and the following expresses the joy he bubbles with
when surrounded by laughing and cheerful children:

I bade a friend good morning,
What's good about it? he replied.
Oh, friend, how can you fail to see,
These children by my side.
Look deep into those trusting eyes,
And you will surely see,
It is the love of our dear God,
Smiling on you and me.

His poetic ability would easily fill a volume, for his
mind harbors a wealth of colorful tales and anecdotes
rich with knowledge and wisdom.

Unfortunately, as is with all good things, the afternoon slipped by all too quickly, and it was soon time
to bid "Adios." The next time I saw Andy, he was on
Main Street bedazzling the mind of a tourist with an
onslaught of choice desert wisdom.

CHAPTER SIX

•

Dominic Lambertucci

My second tenure in Tonopah (1966-67) was the beginning of a long period of learning. Having fled the confines of the city once again, I had embarked upon an unknown world in which I would meet many people, both good and bad. My home in this desert community was a very cozy 42 foot house trailer, approximately ten years old. Lacking the features of late-model mobile homes, my abode was nevertheless a castle for it was comfortably cluttered with shelves of books, boxes of charts and maps, cans of carbide, miner's lamps, coils of rope, two snow tires for my pick-up, and other assorted goods that would gladden the heart of any desert rat.

This mammoth "home on wheels," which I grew quite fond of, was parked at a place known as "Tucci's," or Lambertucci's Trailer Park, the only green spot in a hundred desert miles. Located in Esmeralda County, just a couple miles northwest of Nye County's Tonopah, the delightful oasis had been literally carved out of the harsh land by two Italian brothers, Victor and Dominic Lambertucci, of which only the latter survived.

Upon completion of my day's labor at the local newspaper, I usually headed directly for my trailer-home where I engaged in the nefarious art of bachelor's cooking and then called on Dominic at his gas station/old store complex where he maintained a simple home in the rear. Here in the confines of his kitchen-living-room-dining-parlor we would while away the hours talking about the community, the world, his beloved Italy (which he had not seen for over half a century) and the hopes he held for his many mining claims. He would delight in my passing on a bit of harmless chatter gleaned from the galley proofs at the newspaper, and displayed a smug grin when learning a tidbit of knowledge before the news hit the street via the printed sheet.

Situated at an elevation of 6,000 feet, Tonopah often experiences some excruciating bitter weather, and it was on such nights that Dominic's little home seemed as if it were a Life Station in the wilderness. The light from his window could be seen burning late into the night, for he would stay huddled inside his cozy shelter by an old wood-burning stove. The place had not seen a pail of soap and water in years, but it didn't make any difference. The atmosphere was regal.

Those speaking with Dominic for the first time often thought he "got off the boat yesterday," for his speech was as Italian as spaghetti, but he had been a resident of the Tonopah area since 1913. Shortly after the genesis of my visits, I discovered a truly remarkable man, very sharp and capable of conducting business affairs, but so very naive to some of this country's fast customs. One such example of his lack of knowledge in modern America concerned his gasoline station which dispensed Flying A products. He was probably the last man in America to learn Phillips Petroleum Company purchased the Tidewater works, for he displayed genuine surprise when a customer flashed a Phillips credit card. "Wot ees dis?" querried Dominic. "It's a credit card," replied the customer. "But me Flying A!" he retorted innocently. If it were not for the efforts of his good friend Jerry Kennedy (who often assisted him) Dominic probably would have held his ground and never capitulated. Being interested only in personal letters, he seldom read form mail, including memos from the oil company's head office.

Especially fond of animals, particularly cats and dogs, Dominic would always have a number of such on hand, most all being strays who needed a home. Described as "someofa my friends" these creatures greeted him at every door with an uplifted or wagging tail, lie sprawled about here and there, and generally affixed themselves as integral factors of the Lambertucci household. So great was his love and admiration for these members of his home, that when one cat he called "Bimbo" was hit and killed by a car on the highway, he mourned sorrowfully for days. "My Bimbo, my Bimbo," he lamented. These were his friends, and his love for them was real. They would provide hours of company and companionship in exchange for some food and shelter and a little affection. So unlike questionable human beings, they never betrayed his trusting friendship.

Dominic arrived in this country a few years after his brother Victor had established himself on the desert. I did not have the good fortune personally to know Victor, but he was considered by all as the driving force of the twosome. Tragedy hit the team in 1964 when Victor, then 76 years young, was struck by an automobile as he walked along the highway near his ranch. He died after suffering several days of anguish. The loss hit Dominic hard, for neither brother had married, and the truly remarkable kinship was destroyed. Dominic often journeyed to the nearby cemetery to visit his brother. This was a forlorn spot in the bleak landscape which had been graced with a few trees and shrubs, courtesy of the two brothers.

Alone and often sad, Dominic continued the operation of the ranch without help. He expended a great deal of energy tinkering with a huge Caterpillar tractor, and with the noisy diesel he leveled a large bloc of desert for additional trailer spaces. His yard was cluttered with a varied collection of ancient vehicles, mostly trucks of the flatbed and pick-up variety, each capable of performing some duty on the ranch. And what memories flood the mind when I think of the times he piloted one of the flatbeds into town for the mail and supplies. His machines were noted for their never failing ability to emit resounding backfires and clouds of smoke. The back of his vehicle always supported a dog or two which would bark for all their worth at the local canines, who raced the length of Main Street announcing the arrival of Dominic and Company. Such memorable events will never be replaced with freeways, housing developments, and computers.

The seasoned Italian possessed a truly fantastic 1935 Maytag washing machine and, paying a small fee for water, I often used it. I chose this broken down "old wreck" over the modern laundromats in town, for the two of us stood over it many times discussing its merits while it churned and grunted on a load of clothes. He repeatedly declared "Dey don' maka dem like-a dis no more," to which I could only agree.

Water for the trailer park, as well as the various agricultural goods around the ranch, was obtained from a well some five miles north of the spread, which was powered by a windmill. As winter approached, Dominic urged all residents of the park to purchase "heat tape" and wrap their water pipes, for Tonopah's infamous cold was noted for freezing pipes solid. But many failed to heed the warning for they were products of modern lethargy, and they solved the dilemma by letting the kitchen tap flow all night. Such was nearly drastic, for the reservoir-tank at the windmill could not meet the demand and almost emptied. Dominic worried himself crazy trying to impress people of the problem at hand but, except for a few who knew and understood the ways of the desert, the open taps continued. At one point when the water shortage became severe and a "dry camp" loomed ominously on the immediate horizon, the veteran of the desert was forced to turn off the main valve at night so that the tank might refill. The loudest cry of protest was voiced by those who had ignored Dominic's pleas and had thus created the situation. The majority of these people were city folk who were in the area on government contract jobs.

Throughout the year and despite the weather, Dominic often drove to his well to maintain the workings. It was on one such trip in December of 1967 that he failed to return. The day was bitter cold. After completing his chores, the truck either didn't start or he fell ill. His frozen body was found the next day.

Those who knew him well, truly mourned his passing. Less than a month before his 71st birthday, he was laid to rest by the side of his brother in the Nevada desert — their home for so many years.

Timelessness reigns in the vast solitude of Death Valley.

Mizpah Andy — gentleman, friend, wit, poet and desert man.

The decaying hull of an automobile on the floor of Panamint Valley. The story of its demise is described in the chapter "The Vandal."

The late Dominic Lambertucci, a rare and
wonderful individual.

The author, precariously perched on some timbering,
peers down the shaft of the Bullfrog Mine.

For 50 years the proprietor of a Tonopah, Nevada shoe-shine parlor/tobacco store, this photo shows Charlie Stewart in his shop.

Death Valley is not all sand and heat. Snow and blizzard conditions were encountered when the author first hiked to the summit of 11,049 foot Telescope Peak.

Man not so long ago sought wealth in the mines of Death Valley. It is pathetic that great hopes often end in ruins, as is exemplified here in Chloride City.

Pictured here at Echo Summit, California, Gold Medalist Dick Fosbury executes his now famous "Fosbury Flop."

Dick Fosbury grins in jubilation moments after securing membership on the 1968 U. S. Olympic track team.

Charles "Bill" Blair Jr., survivor of a near-
fatal plunge in the darkness of an abandoned Nevada mine.

Jean Pierre Marquant, adventurous Frenchman as he
appeared moments after completing his summertime
trek through Death Valley.

CHAPTER SEVEN

•

Charles Lincoln Stewart

Long-time residents of Tonopah, Nevada will recall the name Charles Lincoln Stewart with many memories. Proprietor of a combined shoe-shine parlor/tobacco and candy store, Stewart, or "Charlie" as everyone called him, was a member of that mining community for half a century.

Charlie, a Negro, left his native town of Dawson, Georgia in the early years of this century, and eventually made his way to the raw and unpolished mining camp in Central Nevada, arriving on the now dismantled Tonopah and Goldfield Railroad. Stewart often reminisced of that day so long ago: "I remember as though it was yesterday that I got off the train at the old depot and walked uptown," he said in an interview. "I was a smart looking dude in my black button shoes, peg-top trousers, box-back coat and derby hat. My first job, on the same day of my arrival, was oiling the floors at the Episcopal Church and a cleaning job at the Christian Science building. On the following day, April 19, 1913, I went to work for Lee Bell in his shoe shine parlor, and I have been on that corner of Main Street for the full fifty years since."

The parlor which Charlie operated, served many generations of youths as a gathering place — often it was heard among the young men of town, "I'll meet you later at Charlie's place." And so it was, the establishment was a virtual haven for those with idle hours. The narrow but deep shop (not more than 10 feet wide but some 40 feet in length) housed a shine stand, a couple of slot machines, poker table, pin ball machines, and a counter where various sundry items were dispensed. The walls were decorated with mementos of many years and several generations; old photographs of persons of days gone by advertisements of obsolete tobacco products, and other odds and ends gave the place a distinct mark of age.

The late evenings usually found some of the town's old-timers huddled around an ancient radio with Charlie, listening and discussing baseball games. "Whose winnin', Charlie?" was a familiar question of incoming customers. "Yanks, two ta nothin' " was a typical reply. The back of the building invariably found someone mumbling at a pin-ball machine, and a few curses were heard when one of the gaming devices registered "tilt." The lone poker table saw some activity on occasion, although it has been said the "early days" were a lot busier. But the later years (the early 1960's) were usually restricted to penny-ante affairs, engaged in by not-so-serious card fans. I can remember well the evening two fellows borrowed five-cents, entered the game, and in an hour's time cleaned everyone out. They retired with their spoils to the near-by Mizpah Hotel and dined on a New York cut steak.

Some persons of reserved culture might frown on the activities at Charlie's place, but it cannot be denied he helped retard juvenile delinquency by providing a place to go. It was an acknowledged fact, his establishment "kept them off the streets." I cannot remember ever seeing the town constable, aptly dubbed "Barney Fife," being called to Charlie's on business. What few disagreements that erupted among patrons were dispensed in an efficient manner by a firm but collected Stewart.

Possessing an amazing memory for names, dates and faces, Charlie often surprised many an ex-resident who returned to town for a visit by calling them by name and asking of the well being of the family. Some of the youngsters who frequented his shop often tried to "pull the wool over his eyes" by issuing some false claim, but the old-timer who viewed most every form of human being created, was onto them all. He would talk with most anyone who cared to while away the time, and many an impromptu bull session was held there. One could even find a stoic Indian standing about, engrossed in a friendly debate of some sort. Being a Negro, one might think there was tension in this category, but I remember him as a prime example of the "old school" where each treated the other fairly, and both knew the unspoken boundary line of respectability. Never did I hear a word of racial overtone in his shop. I like to think of his place as "the way it should be."

Asked what his main goal in life was, Charlie replied, "I'd like to operate this shop for fifty years —

and then I'd be happy.'' His later years saw him having to ''take a short vacation'' every now and then, for illness prevented him from continuing the daily pace of coping with the steady stream of customers, but he'd always muster strength enough after a few days to return and open shop once again. April of 1963 marked his 50th anniversary in Tonopah and, happy at achieving this plateau, he dropped in at the local newspaper and discussed his life and expressed some of his feeling. ''Fifty years!'' he exclaimed, ''I made it!''

On April 30th, just one week after his newspaper visit, Charles Lincoln Stewart was dead.

I had moved from Tonopah in 1962, but was in town on a visit that day, and was informed of his passing by a friend. I stopped by his shop and peered in through the window. His hat, coat, and that old apron he always wore, hung by the table where he sat. The night light, a pale neon tube, cast an eerie shadow across the small room, and the interior held a weird aura. It was hard to imagine that he was gone, and I couldn't help but think he'd be back to open the door. But no, he was indeed gone, and those who really cared for him mourned. His funeral was one of the largest attended rites held in many years, with several hundred friends paying respect at his final resting place — the dry cemetery on the edge of town.

Charlie is gone, but his spirit lives on in the hearts of the many who knew him.

CHAPTER EIGHT

•

Danger Lurks in Abandoned Mines

The mining camps of yesterday didn't just become ghost towns by some strange quirk of fate, their support was cut off. And in most towns which flourished in the harsh desert country of the Great Basin, support was directly or indirectly attributed to the mines of the vicinity and the amount of good ore which could be extracted from them. With labor disputes, inflation, the great Wall Street panics, and clever maneuvering by international bankers, the very life of many an operation was forced into closure and eventual abandonment with rich ore still available for the taking. With such a turn of events, the mines which once were the centers of teeming activity were left forgotten and dormant.

And so the old workings with horizontal tunnels and surface openings readily accessible are visited by raking winds, a few wild animals, and man — the latter coming to secure salvage for other operations, to explore, and to vandalize. The many miles of tunneling beneath the surface, thousands of miles of it to be sure, now lie dark and deserted and locked in tomb-like stillness. Many are still sound and firm, but with the constant movements of "faults," and Uncle Sam exploding atomic devices deep in the bowels of the earth, most of these old mines are either quite shaky or even caved in.

Often we read in the newspapers of some unfortunate adventurer taking that wrong step and landing a crumpled pile of broken bones at the bottom of some mine shaft. The general attitude of the reader is one of "it always happens to the other guy," and Charles "Bill" Blair, Jr., of Palmdale, California, held this same opinion. An instrument repairman at Edwards Air Force Base, Bill's work often sent him into remote areas of the desert conducting various tests in connection with flight operations for the Air Force. April 24, 1963, was one of those ordinary working days for the government employee, but it proved to be the turning point in his life, as it ended in near tragedy.

The desert was crisp and clear that spring day in April as Bill, then 30 years of age, and a working companion, one "Rock" George, left the Palmdale base and headed for the Beatty-Rhyolite area of Nevada. Bill and his associate had been detailed to the area east of Death Valley to set up speed markers for the famous lady test pilot, Jackie Cochran. A noted pilot of jet aircraft, she was scheduled to fly one of Lockheed's F-104's across the desert sky on a special speed mission, and guidance markers on the desert floor were needed for the flight.

Blair and George arrived at their destination and set to work immediately. By lunch time the pair had completed the major portion of their assignment and decided to hike around the hills a bit after consuming a lunch they had brought along. "Rock," so nicknamed for his avid interest in minerals, promptly became engrossed in an outcropping of interesting ore and had stopped to inspect the formation while Blair ambled up a rocky hillside and began idly browsing about. The area hosted a number of old workings, some indicating large operations at one time, while others were obviously mere prospects. With a curious interest, Bill inspected several of these sites.

"The next thing I did is a bit hazy," Bill recalled in a 1965 interview. He remembers hearing the bark and whine of a dog coming from a mine tunnel and, tracing the sound to one of the nearby workings, ventured into the darkness sans a flashlight or even matches. Proceeding slowly he utilized the light from the tunnel's entrance, and still hearing the barking dog he continued. Having gone about 40 feet the floor of the tunnel was pitch black as a slight jog in the rock walls blocked the meager day light which filtered down the corridor. Still he moved on, seeking the source of the bark, and suddenly plunged down an interior shaft (winze) later measured at 42 feet in depth. In the terrorizing seconds which followed, Bill richocheted from side to side, tore the thick leather jacket he wore to shreds, slammed his head on the hard rock sides, and landed heavily upon one leg atop the dog he had attempted to rescue. The unfortunate animal was killed by the impact of Bill's fall, but the sacrifice saved Bill's life. The animal had broken his fall. Unconscious, Bill lay at the bottom of the black hole more dead than alive.

Meanwhile, on the outside, ''Rock'' looked up from the interesting specimens he had gathered and wondered where Bill had gone. Finding the latter's shoe prints on the tailings of the tunnel, ''Rock'' saw the tell-tale tracks lead into the mine, called to his partner inside, and surmised some trouble had occurred when no reply was received. He hesitated but a few seconds, called a few more times, then departed for the near-by community of Beatty to obtain help.

A rescue party comprised of veteran mining men Dan Kirby and Jerry Lease was formed, and the two men got together the proper gear. Kirby and Lease, accompanied ''Rock'' to the scene of what all feared to be a fatal accident.

With a good source of light the rescue party entered the tunnel and found Blair's prints in some of the powdered dust on the tunnel floor. They followed them directly to the winze, a winch was set up and readied, and Lease was lowered into the hole. He declared Blair dead when he reached him. The latter was removed from the rocky pit in a plastic bag, as was the deceased canine. The ''body'' of Bill was laid upon the ground at the entrance of the tunnel and covered with a blanket. Lease and Kirby, in talking with George, discovered the dog, of a boxer breed, did not belong to either of the two men — which illustrates the fearsome thought that many an animal may have wandered into other such traps. Preparing to remove Blair to a mortuary, the rescurers were indeed surprised to see a vein in his neck twitching. With the situation now different, Blair was carefully transported to the nearest hospital — that being Nye County General, *over 95 miles away!*

Blair's wife was notified of the accident, and hurried to Tonopah as soon as possible. At the hospital she was informed her husband could not possibly survive more than a few days, and was advised to contact the local funeral parlor and have matters taken care of. Reluctantly, Mrs. Blair complied, then prepared for the vigil of waiting. However, somewhere along the line the mine victim didn't "follow the script" for, instead of "cashing in his chips," he improved — to such a degree the funeral director was told to "forget it" and the critically injured Blair was removed to a hospital in Las Vegas, and eventually to one in Encino, California.

Confined to bed for eight weeks, unconscious and with a fractured thigh, Bill's weight of 160 pounds dwindled to a mere 90, his only nourishment being administered intravenously. Despite his lack of consciousness and his leg in a cast, Blair often rose from his bed and attempted to walk around. This resulted in two broken casts. Due to his restlessness, the hospital staff had him restrained with tie-down straps, wherewith his leg mended rapidly due to what doctors called a "clean system." Bill neither smokes nor drinks coffee or liquor.

Approximately three months after the incident Blair had regained consciousness, his broken leg had healed, and he was discharged from the hospital. After additional convalesence at home, Blair was once again quite normal except for the leg upon which he landed. It remained three-quarters of an inch shorter than the other, and a special shoe was required.

Somewhat like the criminal who returns to the scene of the crime, Bill ventured back to the site of his near-fatal plunge in 1965, two years after his ordeal. Going prepared, Bill notified people in the area of his intentions and took a powerful battery operated light; he wanted to see just what he had encountered. Chills raced down his spine as he re-entered the old tunnel; but, intent on observing the winze, he moved on. Cautiously approaching the pit which had caused him so much grief, Bill lay on the tunnel floor and peered into the pit with his light. He was deeply saddened and a bit angered to discover the carcass of *another* dog which had fallen into it.

At Blair's insistance this particular winze was covered with lagging after his 1965 visit, but vandals soon eradicated this effort and left the scene ripe for another tragedy. These persons obsessed with erasing all that is good will be happy to know their work has not been in vain, for in February of 1971 another near-fatal accident occurred. Two men, equipped with only one candle, were exploring this same mine when suddenly there was no floor under one man's feet. He too plunged into the blackness and was critically injured.

In extending a plea of caution, I find the words of Beatty, Nevada's Renee Gibson apropos. Writing in the February 19th (1971) issue of the *Tonopah Times-Bonanza,* Mrs. Gibson in speaking of this mine's two serious accidents stated: "AGAIN — the top of the shaft has been lagged with good strong covering — all we can hope for is that people let it alone; after all he or she just might be the one who gets killed."

A resident of Beatty commented to Blair in 1965, "You shouldn't have gone back to the scene of defeat!" But Blair quickly replied, "I don't consider it defeat for I am alive and well. It's a victory! And now I feel compelled to spread the word to others, warning of these old mines."

A heart-rending lesson, far greater than the public will ever realize, Bill's terrible experience should serve as an example to all who might consider such adventure. Sometimes the price is great, but the message obtained is invaluable.

* * *

Another mine mishap occurred near Tonopah, Nevada in early January 1968, and would certainly have been a fatal accident were it not for the Grace of God.

Thirty-three-year-old Don Anderson, resident of Tonopah and employee of the nearby test range, was enjoying a Sunday outing with friends when the long arm of grief reached out and grabbed him. In the company of several friends the group was enroute to the ghost town of Klondyke, traveling cross country on small displacement motorcycles.

Anderson became temporarily separated from his companions and was returning to the others when his bike topped the dump around an old shaft and plunged

53 feet into darkness. The Nye County Search and Rescue Association was on the scene in a short time and an ordeal which lasted two hours was launched. With the aid of Jimmy Wolfe, Dick Sauer, Dick Rhines and others, Anderson, who regained consciousness at the bottom of the hole, was hauled from the shaft in a wire basket stretcher and taken to a hospital in Bishop, California. With a fractured pelvis and assorted bruises and contusions, Anderson was described as a "very lucky man."

The Anderson and Blair accidents were in shafts less than 75 feet deep, and were just short of being fatal. It is interesting to note many of the desert's old mines are *several hundred* feet in depth and lie open and unadvertised. The main shaft of the Belmont Mine on the eastern side of Tonopah lies with a yawning opening, protected by only a foot-high concrete abutment. Measuring some four by eight feet wide, the shaft is *1,100 feet deep.*

* * *

In my several years of exploring the desert, I have visited a large number of ghost towns and old mines. Extreme caution has been exercised in all my investigations, however dangerous and down-right frightening situations have been encountered nonetheless. Much has been written of "tommy-knockers," the little people who, according to Irish and Cornish folklore, inhabit dangerous mines. It has been said these miners (who worked the West's many mines in years gone by) would quit on the spot when they heard the faint knocking reports coming from the leprechauns, for their assorted array of spine-tingling reports warned of impending disaster. Just a couple of years ago I, too, was greeted by a similar eerie message when in the depths of a rickety old mine shaft.

It was a cold and snowy day in 1967, when some friends and I drove to the little camp of Hannapah in Nye County, Nevada. This particular day the entire area lay buried in several inches of snow, and was silent as some spot on the moon with ghost-like hushness about it. Our unchecked enthusiasm of inspecting old mines led us to one vertical shaft on the edge of the small settlement. I started down the network of ladders, proceeding with a degree of caution which ranged in the "scared" category, for the collar setting and timbering were all soaked with years of dripping water and covered with considerable amounts of moss and algae. I had descended some fifty or sixty feet when I stopped and hung on a time-worn rung of the ladder, listening intently. Deep in the blackness beneath me I heard "tick, click, tap, rap" and other varied sounds which sent the flesh on my back crawling. "What's going on down there Dan?," bellowed an associate on the surface, to which I replied, "the tommy-knockers are here," and I was on my way up. Reaching the surface, we all peered down into the questionable pit and listened again — and they, too, heard the warning of the little people. Generations of miners have relied on these so-called superstitions, and feeling as they did, we promptly crossed that hole off our list.

On a journey into the Silver Peak Range of Nevada (to explore old mines, of course) we were accompanied by a young Paiute Indian from the Tonopah area. On any such venture it is urged that one always include a friend, for danger seems to feast on loners, hence we were happy to have our Indian friend come along. Eventually arriving at a chosen mine of interest, we were preparing to descend an incline shaft when the Indian youth refused to go any farther. Upon questioning we learned he harbored an acute fear of mines, for his father had met a tragic death underground when a dynamite charge exploded prematurely.

* * *

One of the most dangerous mines I've found looked solid and stable at first glance but, as you shall see, it was a potential death trap. This mine obviously was a major operation at one time for it supported a massive headframe, extensive tailing dumps, and a main shaft close to a thousand feet deep. Many mines have good circulatory systems which allow fresh air into the depths, but this excavation consisted almost exclusively of tunnels extending from the main shaft which dead-ended far underground. It was here that a friend and I, garbed in hard hats equipped with carbide lights, ventured to the 400 foot level and found the air extremely stale and thick. The lights of our lamps flickered as if in protest and eventually went out.

Efforts to relight them were difficult but successful, however their operation was poor and feeble. Our bodies were drenched in sweat, and the air about us was as if we were in a tomb. Our steps on the tunnel floors echoed in dull thuds, and sounded as eerie as some midnight horror show in which Boris Karloff would have delighted. It was in this same mine that we found the skeletons and mummified remains of rats and birds — mute testimony to their plight of entering but their inability to find the exit. No words were exchanged between my friend and me. We just glanced at each other, made an abrupt about-face and headed for the main shaft where we could see the tiny square of daylight far above us. Then began the laborious half-hour ascent up the ladders which criss-crossed and straddled the awesome and frightening chasm. Words do not well express the jubilation we felt as we reached the surface, gulped fresh air and felt the security of good old *terra firma*.

* * *

There is also the famous Bullfrog Mine, once a keyword in the language of mining men thoughout the world. Today it lies, like so many of the Great Basin's once-teeming mining centers, silent and nearly forgotten. Located in the Death Valley-Southwestern Nevada region I like so much, I have explored the Bullfrog on numerous occasions, each time noting with misgiving its progressive deterioration. By no means the only visitor, it is obvious other such adventurers did not stop at admiring the various articles of old machinery, but took special delight in destroying as much of the remains as possible.

A few years ago, a friend and I obtained permission of the Bullfrog's owner (Mrs. H. Heisler of Rhyolite) to enter the patented-owned mine to take a series of underground photographs. As we were rooting about looking for choice shots of mine tunnel trackage and ore cars, we stopped our activity and stood in agonizing silence as a deep rumbling came rolling through the earth. We surmised either an earthquake or the atomic test range east of Beatty was responsible. In moments the sound waves moved on through the earth and that "black silence" found only in a mine (or subterranean cave) returned. We later learned the fearful "temblor" was our friend James R. Moffat (author of *Memoirs of an Old-Timer*) piloting his spiffy Studebaker pick-up over the dirt road above to his claims. As most dedicated mining men, Moffat, now deceased, often spent hours just gazing and walking about over his claims, dreaming the sweet thoughts of prosperity.

It was in this same mine, on another visit, that the silence was again shattered. Having established a make-shift base camp near the main shaft in a tunnel on the 150 foot level, we were dining on two very dry peanut butter sandwiches when a horrendous onslaught of rocks and small boulders came crashing down the shaft, tearing away at the wood settings and wiping out sections of ladders. For fear of decapitation we dared not peer up the shaft, but managed to shout an alarm to whoever was in charge of the bombardment. The "rock-fall" ceased, but was replaced by a volley of curses and jeers. When several minutes of quietude had elapsed, I donned my hard hat and headed up the ladders, some now badly damaged, making my anxious climb noticeably more difficult. By the time I reached the surface only a whispering desert breeze greeted me, for not a sign of human life was to be seen. The vast Amargosa Valley to the south produced absolutely zero signs of traffic, but the lingering odor of a cigarette (neither of us smoked) made it obvious our visitor was real and not a crafty poltergeist.

CHAPTER NINE

•

Sierran Olympiad

The month was September and the year 1968. The sports world had its eye focused on the High Sierra and a spot known as Echo Summit. Here, at an elevation of 7,330 feet, some of the finest athletes in America struggled for a position on the United States Olympic Track Team which would travel the following month to Mexico City.

The weather for the entire time of the trials was ideal, and as track and field have long been a favorite with me I was magnetically drawn to the site above Lake Tahoe. Making three such journeys in a week's time from the Reno area to Echo Summit, I recall with nostalgia the pleasant motorcycle rides over the 60 mile course. Unlike the captive feeling one acquires in an automobile, a motorcyclist (with unrestricted visibility) is *part of* the surroundings, and as the machine and I climbed the smooth roadway of Highway 50 toward Lake Tahoe and the Summit, I drank in the beauties of the forest, mountains and Lake. The crisp air which smacked of autumn, was pleasantly startling as the elevation became greater, the smell of the pines pungent and the atmosphere exhilarating! As I look back upon it, fond memories flood my mind and return me to the great times of rounding finely tapered mountain corners at 60 miles per hour. Such moments I shall long treasure.

Arriving at Echo Summit, I shut off the motorcycle's engine and sat in silence and gazed at the natural beauty of the landscape. Here in the hushed stillness of a pine-flecked granite hilltop overlooking Lake Tahoe's casinos, man had carved an Olympic-sized track and undertook the gruelling ordeal of training in the thin air. The setting was chosen because Mexico City, location of the XIX Olympiad, rests at an equally high altitude of over 7,000 feet, and special training is essential in order to cope with the rarefied atmosphere. The site was beautiful but possessed the definite air that the place was a human proving ground.

For weeks the runners, jumpers and throwers sucked the thin air and pushed their bodies to the limit of physical endurance, all for the chance of competing in the finals, and then, if victorious, Mexico City. One event which still lingers in my mind was the finals of the 100-meter dash. I stood near the finish line and watched the eight black men take their places in the "blocks" at the western end of the track. The small crowd uttered not a word and the crystal clear air carried the words of the starter to every listening ear. "To your marks," barked the official . . . "Set!" . . . Blam! sounded the blank pistol, and suddenly the men sprang forward like startled deer. It was fantastic! They pounded down the red turf in a fury of strength and determination — not one made a wasted move — each was in perfect form. The arm and leg muscles rippled and glistened in the afternoon sun, the faces contorted with strain, and the earth fairly shook with the pounding sprinters. In only ten seconds they lunged toward the tape and it was all over. In the moments that followed there was much excitement and happiness among the first three finishers, and muted disappointment among the five who had fallen short. It was a rewarding study in human relations.

Then there was the 3,000 meter steeplechase, a gruelling race which lasted approximately nine minutes and, in the thin air it was nine minutes of torture. The course was over the oval shaped track, but included a standard fixed hurdle (which looked more like an East Berlin roadblock) and a water hazard through which the runners sloshed. A large field of entrants responded to the starting shot, and for the first few laps they jogged in a pack at a rapid pace. Then the lack of oxygen began to take effect. The field "strung out" as the stronger contestants continued the pace and those affected by the altitude felt their stride falter. As the event neared completion, one individual was "lapped" by the others, but the former doggedly plodded onward, striving only to finish even though he knew the cause was lost. The onlookers stood in awed silence and watched this gallant being struggle toward the finish line, his exhausted lungs audibly rasping their anguish. This man was a great runner, probably having won numerous contests in his corner of the world — but now, here in the company of the world's best and under dire conditions, he suffered defeat.

The last day of the trials included the high jump event, a struggle which was thick with human hopes, efforts and pathos. The clear blue cloudless sky and wonderous warmth of the glowing morning sun, mixed with the sweet perfume of the woods, made the spot removed from the world of commercialism a scene of strange beauty.

The field of contenders was comprised of ten men, some in their late teens, and one a senior in high school. But all were mature individuals engaged in the serious business of striving to win and, while each was friendly, all were grim with determination. It was with mixed emotions that I watched the field narrow — the process of elimination steadily reducing the number in a Grim Reaper fashion. Some failed to clear 6' 11'' (itself a fantastic height) but for those who succeeded the bar rose to 7', 7' 1'', and then 7' 2''. At this point only four men remained in the competition — three were Negros or, in today's jargon, blacks, and one a Caucasian. All wanted desperately to make the team, but everyone involved knew only three were eligible for the journey to Mexico. The struggle continued.

Tension filled the air when all four athletes cleared the bar at 7' 2'', and the track officials raised the bar to 7' 3''. At this height, Bill Caruthers of Santa Ana, Calif., sailed over the bar almost effortlessly. Reynoldo Brown of Compton, Calif., followed with the same graceful jump. But then John Hartfield of Houston,

Texas, failed. Hartfield, like Caruthers and Brown was a Negro. His second try was also unsuccessful, and I shall never forget his actions after his third and final effort, for it too was in vain. Kicking the crossarm off the standards as he attempted the jump, the aluminum bar produced an echoing twang which spelled defeat and fluttered into the soft foam rubber pit alongside Hartfield. Lying on his back, Hartfield stared up at the serene sky for the better part of a minute — the world will never know what he was thinking at that moment. He got to his feet slowly and jogged off at a steady pace across the vacant discus field, stopping to talk with no one. The crowd didn't seem aware of him —he had failed, and now exited the stage of trial. I watched him grow smaller as he trotted away, straight and unwavering, until he finally vanished into the darkness of the forest. I could imagine the grief that man was suffering—perhaps he cursed, or prayed, and most probably a tear fell. Only he knows.

But while one man grappled with grief, another was tasting glory for the first time and responded like a youngster on Christmas morning. This was Dick Fosbury of Oregon State University, who possessed a most unorthodox method of jumping. Instead of approaching the jump area in the conventional manner of running toward the bar at an angle, kicking high and rolling over, Fosbury (after rocking to and fro for a minute — in deep concentration) would jog toward the standards straight on, leap with both feet, twist his body in mid-air, and flop over backwards. His execution of the jump is nearly impossible to describe, but so beautiful to watch.

Fosbury's previous best had been seven feet even; so, with his triumph of 7' 3'' and a spot on the Olympic team, he bounced about the sidelines in pure ecstasy, displaying genuine boyish elation with a grin discernible a hundred yards away.

I found in Fosbury's success and his showing of truthful appreciation an ointment for the soul, and in Hartfield's efforts and actions a painful but vivid lesson for the mind and heart.

I have never cared for television and its millwork of "canned laughter" and incessant advertising, but I did view portions of the Olympic Games live (via satellite) from Mexico City. It was pure joy to watch Fosbury, now representing the United States of America, jog toward the high jump bar, leap, twist and flop over at 7' 4 3/4''! He came home with a Gold medal.

CHAPTER TEN

●

Harbingers of Spring

One of the wonderful privileges of living in or near desert country is the many opportunities it presents to observe the remarkable creatures which comprise God's vast kingdom of animals. My residency in Northwestern Nevada resulted in numerous such moments, as I encountered several heart-warming experiences.

Of particular interest was the winter arrival of the Canadian geese.

These beautiful long-necked foul would arrive in huge squadrons much the same as jet aircraft on maneuvers, and many spent the entire winter season in the area while others continued a southern migration after a brief stop-over. Of the various flocks, or however they are classified, I observed a considerable number of them establishing housekeeping on a pond in Verdi, with others in Reno on Virginia Lake (a recreational site in the southwestern portion of that city) and the balance on a lake in Washoe Valley. It was only a matter of time before I began watching them with an intense interest.

Hearing their overhead flight one day, I dashed

from my shop and with a craned neck scanned the heavens and watched the famous "V" formation move across the sky. It was at this time that I became impressed and acutely aware of their enchanting vocabulary, for the gabbling and honking which accompanied their flight was spellbinding. Then one day, as if with a change of directors, an entire fleet passed over my home a mere fifty feet from the ground but without the usual musical chatter. The only sound heard was the rustling wings pumping the wind as they systematically stroked to a distant rendezvous, and gazing up at them I found myself calling out "Beautiful, simply beautiful!"

After a mild snowfall settled on Reno and the sun had returned, I found a contingent of them marching proudly about the city's golf course. The inch of powdery white stuff was obviously a treat to their webbed feet, for the day was warm and comfortable, and their muffled gossiping was like the refreshing sound of a huge choir.

I have often wondered how man can delight in blasting shotgun pellets at these creatures, all in the guise of "sports." Man's sense of value's seem, at least to me, warped.

* * *

As the cold and bitter days of winter faded into spring, I found yet another creature of the wing who brought a smile into my life. This feathered friend would locate on the uppermost branch of my yard's only tree, set up camp and burst forth in a profusion of song. This was Mr. Meadowlark.

Seemingly never stopping for rest, my springtime neighbor would warble all the day long, drenching anyone within earshot with a volley of liquid notes. With my curiosity getting the best of me, I enjoyed a few close-up views of this genius at work with a spotting scope I had on hand. Looking about the countryside as would a king surveying his domain, this remarkable fellow of song opened his bill and rolled forth his message of good cheer from the depths of his soul. Such sounds can soothe the weary and tired heart immeasurably.

The manufactured baubles of man's commercial world can never compare to this truly great artist.

CHAPTER ELEVEN

●

"The Man Who Came to Dinner"

Perhaps the strangest character I ever knew entered my life while I lived south of Reno, in a belt of semi-desert country at the foot of the Sierra Nevadas. Here, where the evenings are usually restfully quiet, I spent countless hours hunched over stacks of books researching interesting historical data and seeking knowledge from the words of great men of the past. Such a pastime is an enjoyable one and quite mentally stimulating, but on occasion it does "get to a fellow," and a break is most welcomed.

It was just such an evening when I was caught between the intriguing lure of my work and silently wishing someone would drop by for a visit, that this strange character made his appearance. Suddenly, out of the darkness and quiet of night, this individual, the most forward I have ever met, was at my front door loudly demanding entrance. I was startled to say the least the first time I heard his verbal outcry. Something inside of me muttered a threat of running off this intruder however, when I flung open the door this bold visitor casually strolled in as I, mutely, stood helplessly by. He wasn't invited to enter; he merely marched in of his own accord, looked around, then demanded food — and likewise in a humble manner, I complied. As if in a trance I stood by and watched as he finished his meal, whereafter he retired to the sofa and settled down for a snooze. Obviously here was a prime example of a genuine freeloader, but I just didn't posses the "umpft" to toss him out.

He awoke from a deep slumber a few hours later, and was given another handout of eats — thus fortified he departed. Good to see him go? You know it! But before the dust had settled, he was back for another round of hospitality. He made it clear that my home was on his list of potential and promising "crash pads" and that if he were treated in a manner to his liking he might be staying awhile. His requirements were simple, but selfish: food, a place to sleep, peace and quiet. Hard to explain, now that I think of it, but his demands were carried out without so much as a complaint on my part. This assuming character accepted my offerings, but never said so much as "thank you," let alone offer to pay for his keep, or work for his board.

Who was he? We might identify him as Mr. Thomas Catt, Esquire.

Strange, isn't it? How a cat will completely take over if you give him half a chance. This next of kin to the lion of the jungle will spend his days prowling about the underbrush of the neighborhood doing what all normal cats do (whatever that is), then return for another session of dining, a nice petting, a chin rub ("scratch just behind the ear, will you pal?") and other comforts a cat finds to his liking.

Independent! The likes of which are hard to compare. Have you ever stopped and wondered how these animals of the wild will stalk, capture and consume smaller animals for food, just like his bigger relatives in Africa, then sit on your lap purring a song of contentment and sleeping in blissful innocence? A dog can be trained to sit at your feet, fetch the newspaper, chase off undesirable company, or any number of odd jobs. But a cat? About the only role he will fill is that of companion, and on his terms. Imposing chap, I dare say!

One day not long after Mr. Catt had established headquarters in my home, he awoke from an afternoon siesta, stretched, groomed himself, then sauntered to the kitchen only to find his feeding dish (an aluminum pie plate) not in the usual spot. It was in the sink. His face displayed a look of perplexity as he sniffed around. Then looking up at me, he emitted a raspy meow as if to say, "What's this, no food? How can this be? Come, come now — let's have a little service!"

Ah, but what a fellow. I'm glad he chose my place. His company was invaluable. When the infamous Washoe Zephyr shrieked like a banshee, and the snow piled against the door with the temperature hovering at ten above, it was rather enjoyable to have the old boy around.

Later, when I became engulfed in a strength-sapping struggle, instigated by an associate, the cat became my only visitor, in that he showed up each evening for food and lodging. Who knows, he may have understood I needed his company. Just as I became attached to the fellow, he came in one night battered, bruised and bleeding. He entered the house with one leg hanging useless, an eye badly puffed, and his entire body marred with signs of battle. Obviously he had met his match. I cared for him the best I could, but he turned down food and attempted to sleep.

The entire next day was spent resting, and the living room had a hushed quiet about it much like a sick ward near a battlefield. The following day he wanted outside. Reluctantly I opened the door and he hobbled away. I called to him as he slowly crossed a field. He stopped, looked back and meowed a reply, then turned and continued on to his unknown goal.

That evening and the many which followed were rather sad and empty — for I never saw him again.

CHAPTER TWELVE

●

The Vandal

Webster defines "vandal" as a "person who, out of malice, destroys or spoils, especially that which is beautiful or artistic." And the desert has felt the sting of the vandal untold times, with both natural and man-made points of interest suffering greatly from this strange breed of individual who delights in destroying.

The Death Valley 49ers Inc., which organized in 1949, has erected a number of historical monuments commerating the Valley's past, a project which has drawn thousands of interested persons. Unfortunately these meritorious endeavors have also been victimized by the vandal, one such incident occurring in 1963. Prior to the November Encampment Days of that year, workers at the Ballarat Junction in Panamint Valley built a stone monument and embedded a bronze plaque, honoring the sun-baked adobe ruins of Ballarat, a ghost town which flourished as a supply center from 1897 to 1917. But before the mortar had set, the vandals, whoever they are, pried the plaque from its foundation and gleefully hauled it off into the sunset.

It's rather difficult to imagine anyone wanting such

a memento, for its metallic value is but a few dollars, and it is doubtful the culprit would display it on his front lawn. As for the committee members in charge of the monument festivities, one can mentally picture their consternation as they arrived at the historic site. The damage rendered by a few can erase the efforts of many.

Last time I looked, the stone monument at the Ballarat turnoff still stood — starkly naked of the intended plaque.

* * *

Those who engage in desert driving have no doubt seen the rusted hull of an old automobile, lying like a skeleton, at the bottom of a cliff or in a flood ravaged gully, soaking up the blazing sun. I have often wondered about such vehicles and have wanted to know the events which led to their demise; but to trace the history of them is nearly impossible.

There is, however, one vehicle I am familiar with which now lies forgotten and deserted on the floor of Panamint Valley. It is either a 1953 or '54 Ford passenger car, once the proud property of some individual but now only a memory. The incident which brought about its downfall occurred in 1960, and I found its "death" another pungent lesson in life.

It was in the Fall of that year when my friend Gary and I were exploring some of the wonders of the massive Panamint Mountains. Defying good sense we drove our automobile up the steep grade of Surprise Canyon into the old mining camp of Panamint City, but in the process damaged the transmission. Not aware of the impending breakdown, we continued our back-country ramblings of seldom used dirt roads and eventually camped in the upper reaches of Wildrose Canyon near the Charcoal Kilns, where the transmission declared a wildcat strike. My companion promptly undertook the task of "pulling the trans" right there in the middle of the wilderness, observed the extracted transmission and decided a new clutch was needed for repair. A long hike to Wildrose Station followed where, after a time, we secured a ride to a parts house in Trona.

And this is where we first encountered the Ford automobile. As we rode with a helpful passerby toward Trona we noticed on the shoulder of the highway the vehicle which I first mentioned. It appeared either to have run out of gas or suffered some mal-function, but like a faithful canine it calmly sat in the afternoon sun waiting for the return of its owner who apparently had gone for help. As we sped by we glanced upon the scene but just as quickly forgot the matter. In Trona we obtained a rebuilt clutch, stuck out our thumbs and started down the road toward Wildrose. Nightfall was soon upon us, but an almost full moon cheerfully brightened the night. It was a beautiful evening, clear, not too cold, serene — but absolutely devoid of any traffic. We walked for what seemed at least four hours. Our pace lagged as our feet tired, but we wearily plodded up the long grade over the Slate Range when an old-timer in an ancient pick-up happened along.

For a few dollars gasoline money the veteran miner agreed to take us to our car — a kind act on his part for it was miles out of his way.

Bouncing along the road in the middle of the night, we passed the Ford passenger car again, still parked where we saw it that afternoon. As we motored by, it looked rather strange in the white light of the moon; but again we paid little attention to it for we had work of our own awaiting us. We eventually reached Wildrose Canyon and our camp site and spent two days laboring and hassling with our car. Our efforts were not entirely successful as trouble still plagued us, but we did get the car going once again. We decided to obtain mechanical assistance either in Trona or China Lake and headed off across the desolate but beautiful Panamint Valley — driving our car with caution.

Once again we approached the disabled Ford but this time we were confronted with an appalling sight. The vandals had struck! I never did meet the owner of the car, but can well imagine the grief which swept over him when he returned to find his car, once a noble piece of transportation, now a jagged mass of worthless metal. The engine had been stripped of the easy-to-get-at parts, the windows broken, tires and wheels stolen, and the owner's personal effects carted off. In the days and weeks that followed the remaining parts that could be salvaged were taken, including the engine block, seats, door handles, and dash fixtures. The car had originally been locked but unattended for not more than a few days; but those persons obsessed with a spirit of thievery had appeared out of nowhere, found the scene irresistable and unleased their emotions on the helpless vehicle.

Now each time I pass that way I usually stop and visit the demolished car and observe its furthering process of decay. My last investigation found that the "cadavar," for that is now what it is, had been set afire, rolled over a number of times, and shot full of holes by enthusiastic sportsmen. Standing in the silence of the huge Panamint Valley, I thought of this modern world which is always holding forums and seminars on brotherhood, peace and admiration for our fellow man. This supposedly universal love in its zeal of extending good will to those on the other side of our planet often overlooks those on the home front. It surely did neglect Panamint Valley that day in 1960.

CHAPTER THIRTEEN

●

"No Atheists in Foxholes"
— or When Stuck in the Desert

In this age of fast living where we hear "knowl-
edged" clergymen doubting the existence of God and
pompously issuing decrees which shove Him a little
further into the background, I found it uplifting to
experience personally the power of God. And my
memorable experience with the Heavenly Father did
not occur in a stained-glass cathedral or some institution of religious education — but rather in the desert,
on the edge of Death Valley and with my pick-up truck
hopelessly mired in the sand.

It was a day which strongly emphasized the approach of summer, and I found myself and my '54
Ford pick-up crawling up a hillside, following one of
those old roads which seemingly trail off into infinity.
The road obviously had not seen any kind of traffic
for a number of years, and didn't even rate recogni-
tion on a topographical map. It was narrow and over-
grown with desert growth, but was passable — until a
point where the roadbed became soft with sand and
loose cinder. Rounding a sharp right hand corner the
old truck quite handily slid off the roadway and

lodged firmly in the soft material of what could be described as a shoulder. Attempts of "rocking" the truck (reverse, then first gear, etc.) proved futile, and the vehicle bored deeper as if settling down for the winter. I bailed out, surveyed the situation and decided a couple boards would have to be inserted beneath the rear wheels. (Have you ever tried to find some planks of wood on the desert?) I hiked all over the surrounding hills for what seemed every minute of an hour before finally locating two very weather beaten and splintered two by eights, the debris of a long-abandoned prospect hole.

Jacking up the vehicle and digging beneath the wheels with a shovel, I inserted the planks, removed the jack and climbed into the cab to back out. Unfortunately, it was not quite that simple, for the wheels merrily spun away, spewing the boards out in a cloud of dust. I repeated the ordeal a number of times, experienced the same results and witnessed the truck nuzzle into the soft cinder and sand until the running board was even with the ground and the wheels completely buried.

All this time I was whispering and muttering a plea to the heavens to "get me outta this mess," but several hours later found only the truck entrenched on a hillside and its driver soaked with sweat and worry — and one can surely become soaked with worry in tight situations. It was over 40 miles to any outside help, the day rather warm and the picture very bleak. And my prayers of "God help me" seemed to drift off into the desert air.

Wearily sitting down upon the ground I was suddenly struck with the realization that I had been "instructing" God to get me out of my plight. Humbly I sat in silence and then asked God to show me what to do. I was immediately hit with what felt like a thunderbolt. Vividly and with clarity I heard an inner-voice say, "Jack up the front of the truck, push it off the jack, repeat the process until it is aimed downhill, give it a shove and jump in." Excitedly I scrambled to my feet, did "as directed" several times, shoveling loose cinder away from the wheels like a frenzied gold-seeker, rocked the truck back and forth, then leaped into the cab and rolled off down through the thick sagebrush. Crashing through and around thick plant life, dodging mine shafts and assessment workings, stirring up jackrabbits which shot off like bullets, I bounced wildly downhill for a better part of a mile until I intersected another little road onto which I turned.

Bringing the truck to a stop I climbed from the cab and without hesitation knelt in the sand and thanked God. It was a rich experience. It proved to me one does not have to be a card-carrying member of some organization in order to reach God.

The desert has been to me an institution of solemn and inspiring education, a region of immeasurable beauty which all but defies description. But it was far from the desert, on a busy Northern California highway in fact, that I experienced a profound lesson that channelled my thinking toward some of the complexities of our age. This incident, which occurred in the Fall of 1969, seared a message deep within my innermost self, as though lightning etched a picture; the impression was of our rapid-paced society and where it is leading us.

Pressures of our modern world and ever-increasing governing structure had at the time amassed for an attack upon my personal life, and as I was seeking and grasping for answers to a myriad of perplexing questions, I was ripe for any meaningful illustration that might present itself. Traveling from the desert country into San Francisco I found the flow of traffic heavy and sluggish until at one point the roadway entered an area where construction was in progress and forward movement ground to a complete stop. Here the tempo became staccato and the air was soon filled with vapors of raw gasoline and choking exhaust. The time was late afternoon and hundreds of vehicles jammed the thoroughfare in the press to reach home. I glanced from my window on several occasions and observed the intent and grim look which the faces of those about me reflected for they all seemed totally obsessed with the grind. Only a motorcycle rider who rumbled by between the rows of creeping automobiles, probably violating some law, seemed complacent, for his face displayed a grin that testified he was an individual free of the mechanized mesh so near him.

At this point my mind began beseeching the subconscious, demanding to know if the world, especially this one about me, possessed any meaning and sensitivity. I struggled with the thoughts, "is this maddening frenetic mass worth it all — are we destined to end our days in a collective slag-heap of burned out and spent humanity?" Then quite suddenly I came upon the scene which electrified my thoughts. On the edge of the highway, mere inches from the passing vehicles, lay a black Labrador retriever—dead. At his side was an Irish setter, conducting a silent vigil. The setter's long red hair was tousled by the turbulent air of the heavy traffic, and his firm nose sniffed first the air then pointed toward the Lab; he looked so proud yet puzzled as he wondered why his fallen comrade did not rise so that they could continue their afternoon jaunt. The setting autumn sun cast a golden hue to the entire landscape, and the faithful setter, caught in the rays, projected a deep golden image which to me displayed a monument of unselfish love, care and child-like-innocence. The crush of progress about me prevented my stopping to pull the stricken animal off the road, so I was forced to move on down the highway with the others, and in short order the pace increased and we all were once again roaring onward to our individual destinations.

For me however, the scene was not one of "out of sight, out of mind," for in the hours, days and months which have since followed I have often wondered at the significance so starkly portrayed in that heart-rending moment. To some it was simply a matter of a dog being hit by a car and killed, but I saw in it a sacrifice where a magnificent animal was destroyed by an object of modern technology, a mechanical device designed for speed and completely void of feeling. To me a message of the utmost clarity had been presented, one with a deep-rooted plea to halt our pell-mell manner of living and turn to a pace in which life is enjoyed as it should be. Flashing through my mind was a picture of this day and age, and what it is really like as compared to what it should be. As I pondered this incident, I found myself thinking how much better it would be if we would reject the maddening rat-race in which most of us are caught—and adopt a mode of living where we can enjoy the seasons, the land, and the many wonderful things our Creator gave us. But I was and still am all too aware of the many ills which plague our land and people, and the changes that *could* be made if those in power willed it.

The system of mass commerce and big business with its requirements that we rush about daily like mad-men, stepping on the toes of friends and business associates, of deceiving those who trust us, of meeting deadlines and punching time clocks, will eventually consume us. Our computerized governing structure is demanding of us our entire thought processes, and it has been stressed from our earliest days of childhood that money is the *only* standard against which all else must be measured. A young man with no collateral save his health and optimism is of small consequence alongside a cigar-chomping, balding, over-fed financial wizard with a brief case full of stocks and bonds. Daily, young couples discover the unpleasant and harsh reality of this system, which is no longer one of free enterprise, when they awaken to their enslavement to long-term time payments made heavy with oppressive interest rates. The United States is now a vastly different country than that which our forefathers created. Even our Constitution, the most wonderful document of government in the world, no longer insures our freedom and the pursuit of happiness, for it has been cut, sliced and trampled upon by men of law who are blind to this country's real needs.

At this writing our nation is engaged in a highly controversial war which has divided the people in an alarming manner, and by the time it finally ceases its bloody mill-work, there is certain to be other problems on which to focus our attention—unless we alter our entire way of life. The battlefields of foreign countries are soaked with the blood of countless American soldiers, and our prisons are crammed with thousands of young men who have puffed a marijuana cigarette, while organized crime and men who are evil to the core continue to roam our cities seeking whom they may devour. When I look upon the ruthlessness of our world, I think of a Bibical passage in Mathew 16:26 which paints a vivid picture for us moderns; it says:

> *"For what is a man profited if he shall*
> *gain the whole world, and lose his own*
> *soul?"*

And this seems exactly what many are striving for — the gaining of the whole world with their hearts becoming cold and indifferent.

As my thinking apparatus becomes jammed with these many thoughts, much like an overloaded circuit board, my mind suddenly flashes back to that incident on the highway. I can still see the magnificent form of that Irish setter, his brilliant hair whipped by the air of the passing vehicles, his stricken friend at his feet with blood streaming from the nose and mouth, and the message of *concern* so impressively shown by the one which remained. Here was an example of an "individual" who cared — could it be that animals are trying to show us something? Perhaps these "lesser creatures" have a message for us all.

So as the yellowish and gray pall of pollution hovers over the many urban centers of this country, and as taxes spiral ever higher, and as tensions mount to the bursting point, and as the threat of subversion both external and internal increases, I extend a plea to those of like thinking to flee this soul destroying realm and transplant ourselves in the country where life is sometimes harsh, but real and beautiful. Let us prepare for the inevitable changes that are coming, changes the likes of which this world has never seen. Seek the beauty and realness of the mountains high, locked in green loftiness — the coastline with awesome waves pounding — and the desert and its mystic charm, for in these natural settings, away from man's strange creations, lie our only hope for sanity — and survival.

Finis

Other Books By Daniel Cronkhite

Death Valley's Victims
The Dreams That Turned to Dust
Ghost Towns of Esmeralda and Nye Counties Nevada

Publications from the Sagebush Press

Memoirs of an Old-Timer
Reviewing Nevada's Legacy
General History and Resources of
Washoe County, Nevada
(A reprint of the 1888 original)